The Question of Free Will

✛

OTHER BOOKS BY MORTON WHITE

The Origin of Dewey's Instrumentalism
Social Thought in America
The Age of Analysis (ed.)
Toward Reunion in Philosophy
Religion, Politics and the Higher Learning
The Intellectual Versus the City (with Lucia White)
Foundations of Historical Knowledge
Science and Sentiment in America
Documents in the History of American Philosophy (ed.)
Pragmatism and the American Mind
The Philosophy of the American Revolution
What Is and What Ought To Be Done
Journeys to the Japanese (with Lucia White)
Philosophy, *The Federalist,* and the Constitution

The Question of Free Will

A HOLISTIC VIEW

✣

Morton White

PRINCETON UNIVERSITY PRESS

Copyright © 1993 by Princeton University Press
Published by Princeton University Press, 41 William Street,
Princeton, New Jersey 08540
In the United Kingdom: Princeton University Press,
Chichester, West Sussex

Library of Congress Cataloging-in-Publication Data

White, Morton Gabriel, 1917–
The question of free will: a holistic view / Morton White.
p.   cm.
Includes index.
ISBN 0-691-03317-X
1. Free will and determinism.   I. Title.
BJ1461.W55   1993   123'.5—dc20   93-7104

This book has been composed in Adobe Utopia

Princeton University Press books are printed on
acid-free paper and meet the guidelines for permanence
and durability of the Committee on Production Guidelines
for Book Longevity of the Council on Library Resources

Printed in the United States of America

2   4   6   8   10   9   7   5   3   1

TO NICK AND STEVE

✦ CONTENTS ✦

I BEGAN to think seriously about free will in the early 1940s, when I was lucky enough to have discussed it with G. E. Moore. In the late 1950s my interest in it was revived as a result of discussions with Isaiah Berlin that have continued to the present day. Although he and I disagree seriously about free will, my exchanges with him in conversation and correspondence have helped me enormously. I therefore thank him warmly for enduring what must have been great disappointment as he read certain parts of my manuscript.

Like any philosopher who has managed to reach my age, I have benefited greatly from reading works on free will by many other philosophers, and I want to use this occasion to mention a few whose writings have been especially beneficial to me while working on this book. These are authors with whom I do not always agree, but the reader knows that agreement is especially rare when the subject is free will, which Hume called "the most contentious question of metaphysics, the most contentious science". As will be evident in the pages to follow, I have been helped greatly by studying the writings of G. E. Moore, A. C. Garnett, Isaiah Berlin, William James, John Locke, J. L. Austin, Donald Davidson, Roderick Chisholm, Aristotle, Peter Van Inwagen, Harry Frankfurt, and Keith Lehrer. And as I am sure that I have forgotten some names that deserve to be on this list, I hope that their living bearers will forgive my sins of omission, and that their dead ones—if such there be—will do the same.

Now I wish to thank those who have been kind enough to have read the whole of my little work in manuscript. As usual, I begin by thanking my wife, Lucia White, for doing what she has been doing for me for more than a half century. She has not only helped me improve my grasp of what I want to say by asking me trenchant questions, but she has shown me how to improve my writing, and she has encouraged me to get on with the job of completing this book.

I also wish to thank several others who have generously taken some of their valuable time to read my work when they might have been reading or doing something far more important and far more interesting. My son Nicholas White went well beyond the call of duty to save me from philosophical confusion and awkwardness of expression. Dagfinn Follesdal persuaded me to try to make what I say here consistent with what I have said elsewhere and what I still believe about related philosophical topics. H. S. Thayer asked me some probing questions that I have attempted, perhaps unsuccessfully, to answer. Jay Atlas meticulously recorded many very helpful reactions to the manuscript and then spent a day with me in Princeton elaborating on them. He, as well as a publisher's anonymous reader, recommended that I deal with a view on free will that I had not considered in an earlier draft, and I wish to express my gratitude to both of them.

Constant revision of my manuscript has led me to require more processing and *re*processing of my words than I thought possible, but no more than my secretary, Ann Tobias, could expertly manage; I am very grateful to her for that.

Princeton, New Jersey
January 8, 1993

The Question of Free Will

Some Preliminary Remarks

ANYONE who asks at the end of the twentieth century what free will is, whether we have it, and how we know that we have it, owes an explanation to those who may wonder why they should read yet another volume devoted to these antique and supposedly antiquated questions. In reply to those who so wonder I should say that my treatment of the subject is distinguished by advocating a combination of ideas that may make this study of interest even to hardened specialists on free will and to those who have studied the long history of philosophical thinking about it. I summarize these ideas in this introductory chapter while fully aware that some of them have been advocated by other philosophers and that no writer on free will can ever be sure that any of his or her ideas on this much-examined subject are absolutely original. I summarize them here even though doing so will make my later elaboration of them more repetitive than I would like it to be. But I do so because I assume that the reader would prefer to know now what he or she is getting into with me, even at the expense of being less surprised later on.

1. A MORAL PRINCIPLE LINKS "OUGHT" AND "CAN"

Suppose that a moral adviser of Cicero tells Cicero that he ought to kill Caesar because Caesar is a tyrant and all tyrants ought to be killed by those who have an opportunity to do so. Does the adviser's statement that Cicero ought to kill Caesar logically imply the statement that Cicero is free to kill Caesar? My answer is that it does not imply it in the sense in which some philosophers might say that the statement that Cicero is a man logically implies that Cicero is an animal. Instead, I believe that the inference from "Cicero ought to kill Caesar" to "Cicero is free to kill Caesar" rests on a moral principle which says that every action that one is morally obligated to perform is an action that one is free to perform. If the adviser assumes this moral principle and the statement that Cicero is morally obligated to kill Caesar, the adviser may of course validly deduce from these two premises that Cicero is free to kill Caesar. But the adviser cannot immediately, on logical grounds alone, deduce the statement that Cicero is free to kill Caesar from the statement that he ought to kill him. Nor can the adviser correctly claim that the conjunction of the statement "Cicero ought to kill Caesar" and "Cicero is not free to kill Caesar" is unintelligible, as some have argued. In rejecting the idea that this conjunction is self-contradictory or unintelligible, I prepare the way for my own affirmative view of the connection between "Ought" and "Can", or between "Ought" and "Free".

In addition to presenting this moral view of the relation between "Ought" and "Free", I deal with the vexed problem of the relation between free will and determinism. I begin by examining the view that "Cicero is free to kill Caesar" logically implies "Cicero can choose to kill Caesar", and that the latter statement logically implies that Cicero's not choosing to kill Caesar is not causally necessitated by anything. After criticizing this attempt at showing that "Cicero is free to kill Caesar" logically implies the falsity of the principle of universal causation or determinism, I then

4

examine a more recent argument for the incompatibility of free will and determinism.

2. AN ASIDE ON THE ANALYTIC AND THE SYNTHETIC

Since I have said that "Cicero ought to kill Caesar" does not logically imply "Cicero is free to kill Caesar" in the sense in which some philosophers say that "Cicero is a man" logically implies "Cicero is an animal", I may appear to be departing from views that I have defended else-where.[1] For it may be thought that by speaking in this way I give my support to the idea that the statement "If Cicero is a man, then Cicero is an animal" is analytic in a sense that I have criticized in other writings whereas "If Cicero ought to kill Caesar, then Cicero is free to kill Caesar" is synthetic. It may also be thought that in stating a view of what "Cicero is free to kill Caesar" *means*—which I will try to do later—I once again fall into a way of speaking that reveals conscious or unconscious acceptance of views of analyticity that I have sometimes attacked rather vehe-mently. For this reason, I want, at the earliest possible mo-ment, to head off the idea that I am backtracking on this important philosophical issue.

I continue to believe that the effort to demarcate sharply between the analytic and the synthetic by resting on al-leged knowledge of the relationship between Platonic con-cepts or meanings is misguided, but I do not think that I am therefore forbidden to use philosophical terminology that is sometimes associated with the doctrine that such a

[1] See my *Toward Reunion in Philosophy* (Cambridge, Mass.: Harvard University Press, 1956), esp. chapters 7, 8, and 9.

demarcation is defensible. In other words, I think that I may say without fear of backtracking that "Cicero ought to kill Caesar" does not logically imply "Cicero is free to kill Caesar" without being committed to the view that a logical implication is true by virtue of the meanings or attributes expressed by the terms in the relevant sentences whereas a nonlogical implication is not. I may say all of this because, in calling an implication "logical" as opposed to "nonlogical" as I did earlier in this chapter, I record my view that it is one that I am very reluctant to surrender as opposed to one that I am not so reluctant to surrender. In other words, I say that the supposedly analytic statement "If Cicero is a man, then Cicero is an animal" is one that I am exceedingly reluctant to surrender whereas the supposedly synthetic statements "If Cicero is a man, then Cicero is a biped" and "If Cicero ought to kill Caesar, then Cicero is free to kill Caesar" are statements that I am less reluctant to surrender in the face of what might appear to be adverse experience.

This gradualistic view is closely connected with the holistic or corporatist theory of knowledge that I espouse, a theory which says that we test our beliefs against experience in conjunctions. So, if the two statements (1) "If Cicero is a man, then Cicero is an animal" and (2) "If Cicero ought to kill Caesar, then Cicero is free to kill Caesar" were both in a conjunction that led logically to a faulty prediction, and if the resulting defect in our conjunctive theory could be repaired by surrendering (1) or (2), then statement (2) would be surrendered and removed from our theory more readily than statement (1) would be. And this epistemological situation would not change in my opinion if one were to call (1) a logically true conditional statement and (2) a morally true conditional statement. I want to assure some of my readers that I continue to think that the distinction between so-called analytic and synthetic statements is best viewed as a matter of degree even though, in an effort to communicate with those who think otherwise, I use their terminology. Although the literature on free will contains terms that reflect the acceptance of views that I reject, I think I can state the issues and offer my own views on free will without lapsing into what I regard as errors regarding analyticity and allied notions. And where I seem to lapse into such errors, I hope that charitable readers will do me the favor of reading my terminology in a manner that will render what I say compatible with what I have said in this section.

3. What Having Free Will Is

It is sometimes said that "Cicero is free to kill Caesar" is synonymous with the statement "If Cicero chooses to kill Caesar, he will kill him",[2] but this view is not accepted by philosophers who rightly say that this conditional statement must be supplemented at least by the statement "Cicero can choose to kill Caesar" if we are to express what "Cicero is free to kill Caesar" means. Some philosophers who insist on such an addition go on to say that "Cicero can choose to kill Caesar" must be interpreted as meaning the same as "Cicero's not choosing to kill Caesar is not causally necessitated by anything". However, in my view, the added possibility-statement that Cicero can choose to kill Caesar need not be interpreted in this antideterministic way. In criticizing this argument for antideterminism,

[2] See G. E. Moore, *Ethics* (repr. London: Oxford University Press, 1949), chapter 6.

I point out that the added possibility-statement should rather be understood to say that Cicero's not choosing to kill Caesar is not causally necessitated by *certain specified things* or by things of *a certain kind*. But this approach need not faze another kind of antideterminist, who says that determinism is to be rejected because it logically implies that whether Cicero chooses to kill Caesar or not, his choosing or his not choosing will be causally necessitated by things that happened before Cicero's birth and over which he has no control. This antideterminist presents an argument against determinism that I shall also consider later on.

Before proceeding any further it will be helpful if I say what I mean by the doctrine that we have free will. I mean simply that human beings are often free to perform actions; and when we say that a particular human being named "Hea" has this freedom, we mean to assert—for reasons that I shall later discuss—the following conjunction: (1) If Hea chooses to perform the action, Hea will perform it; and (2) Hea can choose to perform it; and (3) if Hea chooses not to perform the action, Hea will not perform it; and (4) Hea can choose not to perform it.[3] Here the conjunction of (1) and (2) says that the agent can perform the action; the conjunction of (3) and (4) says that the agent can avoid performing the action; and the conjunction of (1), (2), (3), and (4) says that the agent is free to perform the

---

[3] Locke says "Liberty 'tis plain consists in a Power to do, or not to do; to do, or forbear doing as we *will,*" *Essay Concerning Human Understanding,* ed. P. Nidditch (Oxford: Oxford University Press, 1975), p. 270. And Hume says: "By liberty, then, we can only mean *a power of acting or not acting, according to the determinations of the will;* that is, if we choose to remain at rest, we may; if we choose to move, we also may," Hume, *An Enquiry concerning Human Understanding,* in *Hume's Enquiries,* ed. L. A. Selby-Bigge (Oxford: Oxford University Press, 1902), p. 95. To such statements I add two statements about possibility of *choice.*

action. If we wish to say merely that the agent is free to choose to perform the action, we need only assert the conjunction of (2) and (4). So if we should say that we have free *choice* (by contrast to free will) we mean that human beings often make free choices.

4. How We Know We Have Free Will

As I have already indicated, another of the main ideas employed in this study is an epistemological doctrine that I have elsewhere called "corporatism", a doctrine outlining the method whereby we justify the belief that we have free will as I understand it. This doctrine is closely connected with the holistic view of Pierre Duhem and W. V. Quine that scientists do not usually test isolated beliefs or statements but, rather, bodies or conjunctions of statements or beliefs.[4] However, my corporatism differs from the view of some other holists insofar as I hold that moral beliefs may be included in a tested body of beliefs that also includes nonmoral beliefs. Let us suppose that a philosopher agrees with me that we cannot immediately deduce "Cicero is free to kill Caesar" from "Cicero ought to kill Caesar". If, however, he begins his thinking about free will with premises—some moral and others not—that lead him to make

---

[4] See Quine, "Two Dogmas of Empiricism", *Philosophical Review* 60 (1951), reprinted in Quine, *From a Logical Point of View* (Cambridge, Mass.: Harvard University Press, 1953), pp. 20–46; also Quine, "Five Milestones of Empiricism", in his *Theories and Things* (Cambridge, Mass.: Harvard University Press, 1981), p. 71. For Duhem's views, see his *The Aim and Structure of Physical Theory* (Princeton, N.J.: Princeton University Press, 1954), esp. pp. 187–90. My own view is presented in *What Is and What Ought To Be Done* (New York: Oxford University Press, 1981), esp. chapter 2, but I wish to take this occasion to say that I think my present view of free will is superior to the view I merely outline in that work.

a moral statement like "Cicero ought to kill Caesar", he may infer from this moral statement and the moral principle that all obligatory acts are free the statement "Cicero is free to kill Caesar". This same philosopher, however, may now part company with me and say, as I have remarked earlier, that he can deduce from "Cicero is free to kill Caesar" that Cicero's not choosing to kill Caesar is not causally necessitated by anything. While reasoning in this way such a philosopher accepts a partly descriptive, partly moral body or conjunction of beliefs that should, I contend, meet certain corporatist standards of testing. And I hope to show by applying such standards that this philosopher's conjunction of beliefs should be abandoned in favor of a conjunction that replaces the statement that Cicero can choose to kill Caesar by a denial of a statement that certain specific items causally necessitate Cicero's not choosing to kill Caesar—for example, by a denial of the statement that Cicero's not choosing to kill Caesar is causally necessitated by Cicero's experiencing an attack of a choice-preventing mental disease. I think that such a conjunction is preferable to others for reasons similar to those that make one scientific theory preferable to another.

I hope to show how the ideas I have sketched not only clarify but, I dare say, contribute to the solution of some of the most pressing problems concerning free will. I doubt that what I say will satisfy all readers, but I hope to formulate the main problems concerning free will in a way that will clarify alternative solutions that are open to all of us and call attention to considerations that should be weighed by anyone who proposes a solution. There is, however, no solution to these problems that all persons accept, and the main conclusions to which I come on these matters rest on views about which a consensus may be especially hard to reach. Many widely held views about what the connection is between a moral statement and a statement of freedom, and about how we should understand free action and free choice are views that are neither obvious truths nor deducible from obvious truths. If, however, we adopt a moral version of the principle that "Ought" implies "Free", according to which it may be interpreted differently by different persons, and a related view of the variable meaning of a sentence such as "Cicero can choose to kill Caesar", we may better understand why philosophers find it so hard to agree about the subject of this study.

Like Hume, I think that the question of free will is "the most contentious question of metaphysics, the most contentious science"; but unlike Hume, I do not think that "by liberty . . . we can only mean *a power of acting or not acting, according to the determinations of the* will",[5] since I believe that some determinations of the will or choices must themselves be possible in some sense if we are to have liberty or freedom of action. My method of specifying this sense of "possible choice" leads me to say with William James: "I . . . disclaim openly . . . all pretension to prove . . . that the freedom of the will is true"; and I also agree with James "that its truth ought not to be forced willy-nilly down our indifferent throats".[6] Finally, I should emphasize that although many philosophers have held as I do that all obligatory actions are free, few philosophers maintain as I do that this is a moral principle which need not be accepted by everyone, and that sentences such as "Cicero can choose to kill Caesar" may be expanded and analyzed in ways that may vary with the person who is

[5] Hume, *Enquiry concerning Human Understanding*, p. 95.
[6] William James, "The Dilemma of Determinism", *The Will to Believe and Other Essays in Popular Philosophy* (Cambridge, Mass.: Harvard University Press, 1979), p. 115.

doing the expanding and analyzing. The relativism or plu-ralism that underlies my saying this will, I hope, become clearer later on when I defend my view of the principle that all obligatory actions are free and when I explain the two-step process of expanding and analyzing a sentence such as "Cicero can choose to kill Caesar".

Moral Obligation and Freedom

IN THIS CHAPTER I begin to support my view of the connection between "Ought" and "Free" by criticizing two views about the relationship between a statement that an action is morally obligatory and the statement that it is free. According to one of these two views there is a logical inconsistency in saying that an action is morally obligatory and not freely done; the second view is that it is nonsensical to say that an action is morally obligatory and not freely done. I reject both of these views because I believe that we use a moral principle and not what certain philosophers regard as a logically necessary principle when we infer that an action is free from its being obligatory. In my view this moral principle may be accepted by some societies and not by others, or by some individuals but not by others within a given society or culture. I also believe that different individuals or societies may accept different beliefs that are expressed by means of the sentence "An act is obligatory only if it is free" because they may use the word "free" in different ways that I will explain later on.

1. "HE OUGHT TO DO A" DOES NOT LOGICALLY IMPLY "HE IS FREE TO DO A" OR "HE CAN CHOOSE TO DO A"

Let us imagine that a philosopher believes that the moral obligatoriness of an action logically implies that an agent is free to perform it. And let us also imagine that this philosopher agrees that the statement that the agent is free to perform an action has the same meaning as the long statement "If the agent chooses to perform the action, he will perform it; and he can choose to perform it; and if he chooses not to perform it he will not perform it; and he can choose not to perform it". In addition, let us imagine that this philosopher says that Cicero ought to kill Caesar—that he has a moral obligation or duty to kill him. And let us imagine that this philosopher maintains that this moral statement logically implies that Cicero is free to kill Caesar, which in turn logically implies, according to the above definition of free action, that Cicero can choose to kill Caesar. Because I deny that "Cicero ought to kill Caesar" logically implies "Cicero is free to kill Caesar", I deny that the first step in our philosopher's allegedly deductive argument is valid. His argument moves in what he thinks is a deductive manner from morality to freedom to antideterminism, and I try in this chapter to show that his move from morality to freedom is not deductive.

Because at least one proposed analysis of moral obligation appeals to the notion of possibility or to what can be done, it may seem to permit the sort of deduction that I criticize. I have in mind a version of utilitarianism which says that "Cicero ought to kill Caesar" has the same meaning as "Cicero's killing of Caesar will produce more pleasure than any action that Cicero can perform instead". Suppose it is said that the latter analysans logically implies "Cicero is free to kill Caesar", and therefore that the analysandum "Cicero ought to kill Caesar" logically implies "Cicero is free to kill Caesar". I want to test this view by construing "Cicero is free to kill Caesar" to have the same meaning as "(1) If Cicero chooses to kill Caesar, he will kill him; and (2) Cicero can choose to kill Caesar; and (3) if

Cicero chooses not to kill Caesar, he will not kill him; and (4) Cicero can choose not to kill Caesar". And I want to show that this conjunctive statement is not logically implied by "Cicero ought to kill Caesar" when the latter is interpreted in accordance with the version of utilitarianism mentioned earlier. Since I think that "Cicero ought to kill Caesar" logically implies neither the conjunction of (1) and (2)—which in my view means the same as "Cicero can kill Caesar"—nor the conjunction of (3) and (4)—which in my view means the same as "Cicero can avoid killing Caesar"—I will consider both of these cases separately, beginning with the conjunction of (3) and (4).

In his *Ethics*, G. E. Moore says that when the utilitarian whose views I have presented above says that an obligatory action is one that produces more pleasure than any action that the agent can do instead, the utilitarian *assumes* that he is speaking only of voluntary actions.[1] In this same work, Moore defines a voluntary action as one that the agent can avoid performing, where an action that the agent can avoid performing is in turn defined as one that the agent will not perform if he chooses not to perform it; but in a later work Moore changes his view of avoidability and says that we must add to our definition of an avoidable action that the agent can choose not to perform it.[2] It follows, in accordance with Moore's later version of voluntariness, that when our utilitarian says that an action is obligatory, he assumes that it is an action which the agent will not perform if he chooses not to perform it, *and* that it is one which the agent can choose not to perform. Therefore, the avoidability of the action, as Moore defines it in both his earlier and his later writings, does not

[1] Moore, *Ethics*, pp. 10–12.
[2] *The Philosophy of G. E. Moore*, ed. P. A. Schilpp (Evanston, Ill.: Northwestern University Press, 1942), pp. 623–24.

follow from its being obligatory as defined by our utilitarian; rather it follows trivially from his assumption that his definition of what is obligatory refers only to avoidable actions. Consequently, this utilitarian must not say that "Cicero can avoid killing Caesar"—which means the same as the conjunction of (3) and (4)—follows from "Cicero ought to kill Caesar".

Now let us ask whether the version of utilitarianism we are considering permits the deduction of "Cicero can kill Caesar" from "Cicero ought to kill Caesar". Once again the answer is "No". The statement that Cicero's killing of Caesar will produce more pleasure than any action that Cicero can perform instead does not logically imply that Cicero can kill Caesar. It is logically possible that Cicero's killing of Caesar would produce such pleasure even though it is false that Cicero can kill Caesar. The statement that Cicero ought to kill Caesar does not logically imply the statement that Cicero *can* kill Caesar even if "Cicero ought to kill Caesar" should be held to be synonymous with "Cicero's killing of Caesar will produce more pleasure than any action that Cicero can perform instead of killing Caesar". We must not make the mistake of thinking that by using the phrase "any action that Cicero can perform instead" one logically implies that Cicero can perform his act of killing. This is clear when one says "If Cicero were to kill Caesar, his doing so would produce more pleasure than any action he could perform instead". Obviously, this statement does not logically imply that Cicero can kill Caesar. Imagine that Cicero cannot kill Caesar at that time but that he can kick him instead. It could nevertheless be true that his killing Caesar would produce more pleasure than his kicking him.

I realize that I have cited only one analysis of obligation and one analysis of free action which in conjunction do not permit us to deduce the freedom of an action from its obligatoriness, but I should add that I know of no other plausible pair of analyses of these concepts that permits such a deduction, meaning one that is like the logical deduction of "Kant is unmarried" from "Kant is a bachelor". I am aware that some philosophers might say that the connection between being obligatory and being free is not expressed in an analytic truth but rather in a synthetic necessary truth, a truth they might liken to "Nothing is red and green all over". In that case they might hold that the deductive connection between being obligatory and being free is synthetic and therefore different from the analytic deductive connection between being a man and being an animal, or between being a bachelor and being unmarried. To such philosophers I would say that even if there should be a synthetic necessary truth which allows us to *deduce* that an object is not green all over from the statement that it is red all over, one cannot on similar grounds *deduce* the freedom of an action from its obligatoriness. Though I might grant while using such language that one cannot conceive an object that is both red and green all over, I would deny that one cannot conceive an action which is both obligatory and not free. For I can imagine a people subscribing to a moral code according to which a particular action is obligatory if and only if there is a moral principle which says that actions of a certain kind are obligatory and that the particular action under consideration is of that kind. But the moral code I can imagine here does not and need not contain the principle that every obligatory action is free, neither as a logically necessary principle which is analytic nor as one which is synthetic and which allegedly permits one to say that "Cicero ought to kill Caesar" logically implies "Cicero is free to kill Caesar". In other words, I do not think that every moral code must, by virtue

17

of being a moral code, contain the principle that every morally obligatory choice is free.

However, I have said that one may make a nondeductive inference from "Cicero ought to kill Caesar" to "Cicero is free to kill Caesar" if one's moral code does contain the moral principle "Whatever action one is obligated to perform one is free to perform". This moral principle may not have the same form as moral principles in the Ten Commandments, which assert that acts of a certain kind ought or ought not to be done, but it is as much a moral principle as they are because it, like them, links a descriptive predicate, "action that one is free to perform", with a moral predicate, "action that one is obligated to perform". If we consider its logical equivalent, "Whatever action one is not free to perform one is not obligated to perform", we may be more readily persuaded that it is a moral principle which supports the inference we are considering here. This is what I have in mind when I say that we may regard the inference from "Cicero ought to kill Caesar" to "Cicero is free to kill Caesar" as morally valid even though it is not logically valid, and also what I have in mind when I say that the former statement morally implies the latter. The inference is not logically valid, just as the inference from "This is water" to "This boils at one hundred degrees centigrade" is not logically valid but, as we might say, physically valid because it depends on the acceptance of a physical law. Moreover, if we accept the statement that "Cicero is free to kill Caesar" logically implies "Cicero can choose to kill Caesar", we may also accept the moral principle, "Whatever action one ought to perform one can choose to perform."

Both of the principles: "Whatever choice one ought to make, one can make" and "Whatever action one ought to perform, one can perform", are moral because they link obligatoriness with descriptive attributes just as other moral principles do. And although I accept them and am reluctant to surrender them, I am more reluctant to surrender principles of formal logic and statements like "Every bachelor is unmarried". I repeat, however, that I can imagine societies in which these moral principles are not accepted and that people would not accept the principle that all obligatory actions are free if they believed that actions are obligatory if and only if they fall under the principles listed in the Ten Commandments. In a society subscribing to that kind of morality, one would not be relieved of a duty to perform an action if one were not free to perform it; according to such a morality, one would say that even a robbery committed by a kleptomaniac ought not be committed. Because I can *imagine* a morality or moral code like that, I find it difficult to attribute the universality that some philosophers attribute to the principle that "Ought" implies "Free". Historians might say that such a morality is more than imaginary because there have been societies which have rejected the dictum that "Ought" implies "Free". My own claim, however, is weaker than that. I merely assert that *there could be* such a morality. And if it is said that the step from the moral obligatoriness to the freedom of an action is a deductive step on the way to proving that determinism is false, then if I show that it is not a deductive step, but *at best* a moral step which rests on a principle that need not be universally accepted, I have removed one link from the deductive chain that allegedly leads from morality to the falsity of determinism.

I have elsewhere suggested that the relationship between "Mr. Hea's action is obligatory" and "Mr. Hea's action is free" is that of presupposition in a sense similar to one developed by P. F. Strawson. He says that you presuppose the existence of the children of Queen Elizabeth if you make a true-or-false statement by uttering the words "All of Queen Elizabeth's children are asleep". In other words, Queen Elizabeth's having children is a necessary condition for making true-or-false statements by the use of the above sentence. However, I have argued that even if we presuppose the existence of the Queen's children when making the true-or-false statement "All of Queen Elizabeth's children are asleep", we cannot *prove* that she has children by deducing their existence from the statement that this is a true-or-false statement. Analogously, we cannot prove that Mr. Hea's action is free by arguing that we presuppose its freedom when we make a true-or-false statement by uttering the words "Mr. Hea's action is obligatory". To show that Mr. Hea's obligatory action is free we must engage in another kind of inquiry.[3]

2. THE CONJUNCTION OF "HE OUGHT TO DO A" WITH "HE IS NOT FREE TO DO A" OR WITH "HE CANNOT CHOOSE TO DO A" IS NOT NONSENSICAL

So far I have considered the view that "Mr. Hea's action is obligatory" logically implies "Mr. Hea's action is free", and the view that the first statement presupposes the second. Now I want to examine the view that the conjunction of a singular "ought"-statement about an action and the denial that the agent can choose to perform that action is unintelligible rather than contradictory. A philosopher who adopts this view in order to call the doctrine of universal causal necessitation or determinism into question would

---

[3] See my *Foundations of Historical Knowledge* (New York: Harper and Row, 1965), pp. 280–81; also P. F. Strawson, *Introduction to Logical Theory* (New York: John Wiley & Sons, 1952), pp. 175–79.

say that the conjunction of the statement that Cicero cannot choose to kill Caesar and the statement that he ought
to kill Caesar is not logically false but unintelligible. From
this such a philosopher might conclude that the conjunction of the doctrine of determinism and the statement that
Cicero ought to perform the action is also unintelligible.
So, in order to avoid such unintelligibility, this philosopher thinks he should surrender determinism, presumably
because he would rather assert singular statements of
moral obligation than the principle of determinism.

In my view, this argument from unintelligibility or
meaninglessness is no more effective than the argument
from contradictoriness. Some philosophers might hold
that asserting "Cicero ought to kill Caesar" when Cicero
cannot choose to kill Caesar is unintelligible because it is
like saying that a stone ought to fall even though the stone
cannot choose to fall. Their point is that we should not
make a moral "ought"-statement about the falling of the
stone for the same reason that we should not make a moral
"ought"-statement about Cicero's killing of Caesar if Cicero cannot choose to kill Caesar. Since it is nonsensical to
say of the falling of the stone that it ought to be performed
by the stone, so—it is argued—it is nonsensical to say of
Cicero's killing of Caesar that it is an action that ought to
be performed by Cicero at a time when he cannot choose
to do so. However, a stone's falling to the ground is not an
action as the word "action" is understood by moralists
whereas Cicero's killing of Caesar *is* an action. Moreover,
the fact that the latter is an action does not make it a free
action for philosophers who define "free action" so that
some actions turn out to be free and others not free, and
therefore the question at issue is whether it is nonsense to
say that an unfree action ought to be performed. I believe
that it is not nonsense; I maintain that a person may speak

intelligibly when passing such a moral judgment on an admittedly nonfree human action.

Of course, I know that there is more to be said about the difference between a nonaction such as a person's fall (as opposed to a jump) from an airplane and an unfree human action such as a person's stealing a gold watch because he is undergoing an attack of kleptomania. I agree that we would be said to speak nonsensically if we were to say "Mr. Hea ought not to have fallen this morning", meaning that he had a moral obligation not to fall. But I don't think we would be said to speak nonsensically if we were to say "Mr. Hea ought not to have stolen that gold watch this morning" when we knew that Hea stole it because he was having an attack of kleptomania and therefore could not choose not to steal the watch. It would not be meaningful to say "Mr. Hea performed the action of falling from the plane" whereas it would be meaningful to say "Mr. Hea performed the action of stealing a gold watch". The fact that Mr. Hea stole the watch because he was having an attack of kleptomania might lead us to say that the statement that Hea had an obligation *not* to have stolen the watch was *false*, but I don't think that our knowing that he had an attack of kleptomania would make it *nonsensical* to say "Hea ought not to have stolen the watch". Furthermore, some moral judges (in our society or in others) might insist that Hea ought not to have stolen the watch because they do not think that having an attack of kleptomania removes Hea's duty not to steal.[4] I realize that it may be difficult to

---

[4] See Alan R. White, *Modal Thinking* (Ithaca, N.Y.: Cornell University Press, 1975) "It is not unusual or odd that someone cannot do what he ought to do . . .", p. 147. I should add here that I think it correct to say that the expression "removes Hea's duty not to steal" may sometimes be replaced by "excuses Hea from the duty not to steal". But I have been persuaded by Jay Atlas that sometimes when we use the expression "excuses

draw the line between a nonaction such as Hea's fall from the plane and Hea's kleptomaniacal act of theft, but I think that philosophers who distinguish free from unfree actions depend on the existence of such a line when thinking of these matters. Falling and becoming a year older are different in a crucial way from jumping and stealing.

In order to give further support for my view, I ask the reader to imagine that a moral judge knows, or claims to know, that Cicero cannot choose to kill Caesar at a certain time because at that time he is suffering an attack of a choice-preventing disease such as epileptic automatism. In spite of this, I claim, the moral judge may believe that Cicero has a duty to kill Caesar at that time because (1) the moral judge accepts without qualification the principle "Every citizen has a duty to kill a tyrant when he has the opportunity to do so", and (2) the moral judge means by the phrase "has the opportunity to do so" that the citizen is in a position to do so without implying that the citizen can choose to do so. Imagine, too, that this moral judge also asserts that Cicero is a citizen who has the opportunity to kill Caesar and that Caesar is a tyrant and that from his premises the moral judge deduces that Cicero has a duty to kill Caesar at the time in question. Can we reject his conclusion merely by saying that anyone who assigns this duty to Cicero at a time when he also says that Cicero cannot choose to kill him is speaking unintelligibly? I confess that I do not see how, so long as the moral judge holds that the singular moral statement is supported by appealing to his stern moral principle and the mentioned singular de-

---

Hea from the duty not to steal", we do *not* intend to say that Hea's duty has been removed but rather that Hea has been exempted from performing it, in which case we may say that he still has the duty. I use "excuse" in the first way when I say that a kleptomaniac is excused from the duty not to steal.

scriptive statements, no one of which states that Cicero *could* choose to kill Caesar but one of which states that Cicero had the opportunity to kill Caesar inasmuch as he had a weapon, was close enough to Caesar, did not have his vision blocked, and so on. We may think it morally wrong of this stern moralist to impose such an absolute duty on Cicero while he is suffering his attack of epileptic automatism, and therefore we may say that because Cicero is suffering his attack, he does not have a moral duty to kill Caesar since he is relieved of that duty. But in saying that he is relieved of it, are we not appealing to our own moral principle? We may object to the stern moralist's principle because it does not contain the qualification that the citizen can choose to kill the tyrant, and therefore we may say that if the moralist's principle had contained that qualification, the moralist would not have been able to deduce that Cicero had a duty to kill Caesar at the time in question because his descriptive premises—"Cicero is a citizen", "Caesar is a tyrant", and "Cicero had the opportunity to kill Caesar"—did not include the supposedly false statement that Cicero could choose to kill the tyrant. But we do not make this objection by appealing only to semantical considerations. We do not say that the stern moralist has violated some philosophical criterion of meaning or intelligibility. Instead, we propose a way of improving the stern moralist's moral principle so that it becomes more like one to which we subscribe. And this, I believe, shows that a moralist who says that Cicero has a moral duty to kill the tyrant Caesar even though Cicero is undergoing an attack of a choice-preventing disease is in our view a candidate for moral improvement and not a candidate for instruction in the philosophy of language.

Of course, it might be replied that the addition of the qualification that the citizen can choose to kill a certain person is a special kind of qualification of our moral principle, that it is different from what might be called a normal qualification that might be illustrated as follows. Suppose that a moralist first accepts the principle "No person ought to kill another person" but later qualifies it so that he instead says, "No person ought to kill another person who has not tried to kill him". Here the supposedly normal qualification, made to avoid making killing in self-defense a moral crime, might be said to be fundamentally different from the supposedly abnormal qualification that is made in our earlier illustration when we add to the subject-term of our moral principle that the agent can choose to kill the tyrant. But how is it different? In the earlier case of qualification we begin with the moral principle: "Whenever a citizen has the opportunity to kill a tyrant, he ought to kill him". We are then led to say instead: "Whenever a citizen has the opportunity to kill a tyrant *and, in addition, can choose to kill him*, that citizen ought to kill him". In the later case we begin with the principle "No person ought to kill another person", and this time we are led to say instead: "No person ought to kill another person *who has not tried to kill him [the first person]*".

Now we may ask whether the two qualifications represented by the italicized expressions differ in a fundamental way. Would those who hold the view I am criticizing say that in the first case adding the phrase "and, in addition, can choose to kill him" is necessary in order *to make sense* of the unrevised principle, whereas in the second case the addition of the phrase "who has not tried to kill him (the first person)" is *not* necessary in order to make sense of the unrevised principle? I deny this because I believe that I *understand* both unrevised principles and because I believe that correcting the first one in the described manner—like correcting the second one in the described manner—does not change it from an unintelligible principle to an intelligible one but rather from an unacceptable moral principle to a supposedly acceptable one. The progress is not from nonsense to sense but from a principle that is, as we think, not acceptable to one that *is* acceptable, or at least more acceptable.

I want to add that I have arrived at my present moral version of the relationship between singular "ought"-statements and singular "can"-statements such as "Cicero ought to kill Caesar" and "Cicero can kill Caesar" after a long period during which I viewed the underlying principle differently. I once thought that this principle was metalinguistic because it said that we have a moral duty to apply a moral word such as "obligatory" or "wrong" to an action only if the action were free or could be performed. But now I think that this ascent into the moral metalanguage of morals is unnecessary, and I think that it would not serve a useful purpose here to give an account of the reasons for my change of mind. What the dictum—which I now regard as a first-level moral law or principle—says is simply that an act is obligatory only if it is free, and therefore that an act is not obligatory if it is not free.

3. "LIBERTY . . . IS THE POWER A MAN HAS TO DO OR FORBEAR DOING", LOCKE

It will be recalled that I have said that a person is free to perform an action if and only if that person performs the action if he chooses to perform it, does not perform the action if he chooses not to perform it, can choose to perform it, and can choose not to perform it. Consequently, in saying that a person ought to perform an action only if that person is free to perform it, we must keep in mind this four-conjunct analysis of "free" (whose conjuncts appear in an order which differs from that in which they have appeared earlier). Here I want to show why we need to add the second conditional conjunct, leaving for later discussion the reason for adding the other conjuncts.

Consider the case where we merely use the first conjunct and say that Cicero is free to kill Caesar if and only if Cicero will kill Caesar if Cicero chooses to do so. It may be, in accordance with what Harry Frankfurt has argued, that an external force will also, by itself, cause Cicero to kill Caesar.[5] Such a situation would illustrate what John Stuart Mill calls the plurality of causes, as when a man dies as a causal consequence of being shot and of being stabbed simultaneously. It also illustrates what is called "overdetermination", where an effect is determined or causally necessitated by more than one cause. In such a case we may assert that Cicero's choice will bring about his killing of Caesar but also that he will kill Caesar even if he does not choose to kill Caesar. If there is an external force that will of itself cause Cicero to kill Caesar, he will kill him no matter what he chooses to do. Shouldn't we wonder, therefore, whether we should say in that case that he is *free* to kill Caesar?

Our puzzlement here leads to other puzzles. Suppose we think that a person is morally responsible for an action if and only if he is free to perform it. And suppose we say "If Cicero chooses to kill Caesar, he will kill him" means the same as "Cicero is free to kill Caesar". In that case we will say that Cicero is morally responsible for killing Caesar if and only if it is true that if Cicero chooses to kill Caesar, he

[5] H. Frankfurt, "Alternate Possibilities and Moral Responsibility", *Journal of Philosophy* 66 (1969): 829–39.

will kill him. Therefore, we will be faced with the problem that worries Frankfurt, since we will have to say that Cicero will be morally responsible for killing Caesar even if his killing him will be brought about by an external force. We will regard him as morally responsible for killing Caesar even though he cannot do otherwise.

All of this leads me to think—with Locke, as we shall soon see—that we should add the second conditional conjunct to our analysans for "Cicero is free to kill Caesar". If we are worried that a supposed external force will of itself cause Cicero's killing of Caesar at the time at which Cicero himself will cause it by choosing to kill Caesar, we can take care of the difficulty that worries us by adding "If Cicero chooses not to kill Caesar, he will not kill him" to our analysans. By making this addition, we imply that Cicero's choosing *not* to kill Caesar will bring about his *not* killing Caesar and therefore we imply that there is no external force that will of itself bring about Cicero's killing of Caesar. There will not be such an external force if our enlarged definition of free action implies not only that Cicero can kill Caesar but also that he can avoid killing Caesar. Just as the statement that Cicero has the power to kill Caesar implies that there is no external force which will cause Cicero *not to kill* Caesar, so the statement that Cicero has the power not to kill Caesar implies there is no external force which *will* cause Cicero to kill Caesar. Transferring this to the case where Brutus has already chosen to kill Caesar and therefore killed him, we may say that had he chosen not to kill Caesar, he would not have killed him, in which case there was no external force that caused Brutus to kill Caesar.

The history of reflection on free will being as long and as repetitious as it is, we should not be surprised to find that Locke said something that bears directly on the issue. In his *Essay*, Locke imagines that a man, while fast asleep, is transported to a room in which he meets, when he wakes up, a person whom he is happy to be with. Consequently, he chooses to stay and therefore does stay in the room. However, unbeknownst to him, the room is locked in a way that precludes his leaving, so he has to stay. Here we have a situation that is virtually the same as the situation we have previously described. It is true that the man stays because he chooses to stay and also true that an external force—locking him in a room—causes him to stay. There-fore, one might infer that he can stay and hence is morally responsible for staying, and also infer that he is forced to stay and hence is not morally responsible for staying. To his credit, Locke concludes on the basis of his illustration that to analyze "He is free to do it", one must say that the agent can perform the action and can avoid performing it, for this will make clear that the man locked in the room did not have the liberty to stay, which, Locke thinks, is the power both to stay and not to stay.[6]

If we therefore say that a person is morally responsible for performing an action if and only if that person can per-form the action and can refrain from performing it, we may ask how this affects the principle that if a person ought to perform an action, then that person is morally responsible for it. Obviously, we must say that if a person ought to perform an action, then that person can perform the action and can refrain from performing it. (Let us leave aside for the moment the question whether the person can *choose* to perform the action and the question whether the person can *choose* to refrain from performing it). It will follow that a person will not have an obligation to perform

---

[6] Locke, *Essay Concerning Human Understanding*, p. 238. Also see Donald Davidson, "Freedom to Act", *Essays on Actions and Events* (Ox-ford: Oxford University Press, 1980) pp. 74–75.

the action if he cannot perform the action or if he cannot refrain from performing it. By saying that the agent's obligation can be removed in either one of two ways, we imply that Locke's man in the locked room does *not* have an obligation to stay because he does not have the power not to stay and therefore does not have the liberty to stay. It may seem paradoxical to say that the man does not have the liberty to stay when it is true that he will stay if he chooses, but so saying is a consequence of our desire to avoid other paradoxical ways of speaking. For if we do not add to our analysis of free action that if he chooses not to stay, he will not stay, we will have to agree that the man in the locked room has an obligation to stay there even though he *has* to stay there. But this seems to go against the idea that if he ought to stay, it is not true that he (physically) must stay—the idea that he has no duty to do what he cannot avoid doing. Therefore, I am inclined to say that if a person ought to perform an action, then that person can perform it and can refrain from performing it.

IF I also say—as I do—that an agent who can perform an action can choose to perform it, and that an agent who can refrain from performing it can choose not to perform it, the reader may well ask me what I mean by saying that the agent *can* make these choices. In dealing with this question in the next chapter, I reject the view that we *must* accept antideterminism as a consequence of the correct analysis of the statement that the agent can make these choices. I also deny that a correct analysis of it requires us to accept determinism. In the language of William James, I hope to show that neither the truth of determinism nor the truth of antideterminism can be logically forced down our throats when we say that we have free will. Of course

I do not maintain that both determinism and its contradictory, antideterminism, are false. But I do maintain that we need not commit ourselves about their truth or falsity in asserting that we have free will.

The Relativity of Freedom

HAVING EXAMINED a dubious route by which some philosophers move from "Cicero ought to kill Caesar" to "Cicero is free to kill Caesar", I now want to examine an equally dubious route by which some philosophers try to deduce the denial of determinism from "Cicero is free to kill Caesar". I do not question their statement that "Cicero is free to kill Caesar" implies "Cicero can choose to kill Caesar" by virtue of an analysis of free action, but I do question their statement that "Cicero can choose to kill Caesar" must be replaced by "Cicero's not making the choice of killing Caesar is not causally necessitated by any other event". Therefore, I want to propose another way of interpreting "Cicero can choose to kill Caesar". But before making my proposal, I want to comment on two unsuccessful attempts to accomplish this.

1. SOME UNSUCCESSFUL EFFORTS TO RENDER FREE CHOICE COMPATIBLE WITH DETERMINISM

Some philosophers under the influence of Moore may fall into the trap of saying that "Cicero can choose to kill Caesar" means the same as the conditional statement, "If Cicero chooses to choose to kill Caesar, he will choose to kill Caesar", thereby launching an objectionable regress. For if the possibility-statement "Cicero can kill Caesar" is not equivalent to "If Cicero chooses to kill Caesar, he will kill him" alone because we must add the statement "It is possible for Cicero to choose to kill Caesar", then if we say that this added statement of possibility has the same meaning as yet another conditional statement—namely, "If Cicero chooses to choose to kill Caesar, then Cicero will choose to kill Caesar"—we will have to assert the possibility of Cicero's choosing to choose to kill Caesar, and so on indefinitely.[1]

In what I think is another unsuccessful attempt to interpret an assertion of the possibility of a person's making a certain choice, Moore says that "one of the commonest senses of the word 'possible' is that in which we call an event 'possible' when no man can *know for certain* that it will *not* happen".[2] Moore does not see any difficulty in holding that we may employ "possible" in this sense when saying that it is possible for Cicero to choose to kill Caesar. But how should we analyze the statement that a particular man cannot know for certain that Cicero will not choose to kill Caesar? Moore does not tell us, but it is well to warn against analyzing "Cicero cannot know for certain that Cicero will not choose to kill Caesar" as having the same meaning as "If Cicero tries to learn whether Cicero will not choose to kill Caesar, Cicero will not come to know for certain that Cicero will not choose to kill him". For in that case we will have to add that Cicero *can* try to learn whether Cicero will not choose to kill Caesar, and we will be faced with the problem of eliminating the expression "can try to learn". Here we use the expression "can try to learn" in an effort to analyze what we mean by the phrase "can choose to kill", but we make no philosophical prog-

---

[1] See Moore, *Ethics*, pp. 135–36; also see Peter Van Inwagen, *An Essay on Free Will* (Oxford: Oxford University Press, 1983), pp. 114–26, for some arguments against this view.

[2] Moore, *Ethics*, p. 136.

ress if we proceed in this way, since the "can" in "can try to learn" is as much in need of clarification as the "can" in "can choose to kill". And if we do not present any other analysis, we will have to contend with the unanalyzed "can" in Moore's expression "can know for certain", a "can" which is as problematic on its face as the "can" in "can choose to kill".

Although I think this second attempt by Moore suffers from the defects I have mentioned, I do not dismiss it on the ground that this use of "can" and a related use of "could" are vulgarisms, as J. L. Austin comes close to doing.[3] Let us consider a case like that which Moore discusses, where we say "Cicero could have chosen to perform act *A*", or "It was possible for Cicero to choose to perform act *A*". If we interpret these sentences as meaning that no man could know for certain that Cicero would not so choose, Austin seems to think that we wrongly treat them as though they meant the same as "Cicero *might* have chosen to perform act *A*". But Austin's suggestion that "Cicero could have chosen to perform act *A*"—when so understood—is a vulgarism does not invalidate Moore's point, which is to challenge us to show that "No man could have known for certain that Cicero would not choose to perform act *A*" does *not* mean what some philosophers mean when they say "Cicero could have chosen to perform act *A*". Philosophers often speak with the vulgar, and therefore we should not rule out Moore's suggestion that this epistemic interpretation of "Cicero could have chosen to perform act *A*" captures what some philosophers have in mind when they make such a statement while trying to show that free choice is logically compatible with determinism.

[3] J. L. Austin, *Philosophical Papers* (Oxford: Oxford University Press, 1961), p. 155.

It seems to me, however, that we may test the acceptability of this suggestion by asking whether the statement "Cicero could not have chosen to perform A" when so interpreted morally implies—in the sense I have previously explained—that Cicero did not have an obligation to perform A. Suppose we think that Cicero had a moral obligation to kill Caesar and later we learn that someone could have known for certain beforehand that Cicero would not make this choice, and from this conclude that Cicero could not make it. Would we on this account deny the statement that Cicero had a moral obligation to kill Caesar? I do not think that we would, and for this reason I am inclined to think that the epistemic view of "Cicero could have chosen to kill Caesar" is not adequate in the contexts that concern us. The statement that some person could have known for certain beforehand that Cicero would not make a certain choice does not seem to constitute the analysis of the statement that Cicero could not make that choice, and therefore the statement that no person could have known for certain beforehand that Cicero would not make the choice does not seem to constitute the analysis of the statement that Cicero $could$ make that choice. And, in any case, it is fair to point out what we have seen in the analogous case of "can choose" and "can know", namely, that the analysans here contains the phrase "could have known" and for that reason alone is unsatisfactory when we are trying to analyze "could have chosen" because of a doubt about the meaning of "could have".

One more point about this epistemic view of possible choice. Moore says that almost always, when we have made a choice, it was possible that we should have chosen differently in the sense that no man could know for certain that we should not so choose. This implies that almost all of our choices are possible, and therefore that it will rarely be the case that a choice is not obligatory on the score of being one that is impossible. In my opinion, this represents a departure from the way in which we ordinarily speak and think since we do say and think that many choices are impossible and therefore not obligatory. This, I think, is a strong argument against the view that *all* choices are possible and against the view that *most* choices are possible.

2. HOW SHOULD WE INTERPRET "CICERO CAN CHOOSE TO KILL CAESAR"?

In spite of the shortcomings of the epistemic interpretation, it is of interest for reasons that I want to discuss briefly before making a proposal about how to understand such sentences. First of all, the epistemic interpretation is offered by Moore in the spirit in which I shall offer my own. He asks advocates of free will who think that free will implies the possibility of choice whether they can show that his epistemic analysis of "Cicero can choose to perform act *A*" is *not* correct. Secondly, his analysis bears an interesting structural relationship to an analysis that I find appealing, so that a few more words about his view may provide an illuminating transition to my own. If, with Moore, we offer, as an analysis of "Cicero can choose in the coming second to kill Caesar", the statement "No man can know for certain that Cicero will not choose to kill Caesar in the coming second", we may derive from it its equivalent: "It is not the case that some man can know for certain that Cicero will not choose to kill Caesar in the coming second". And this statement bears an interesting structural resemblance to "It is not the case that some event of kind K causally necessitates that Cicero will not choose to kill Caesar in the coming second", which provides the form for what I think may be an acceptable view of how to interpret "Cicero can choose to kill Caesar". The important thing to notice is that the assertion of the possibility of Cicero's choice is linked in both cases with the denial of an existential statement—denying in the first case that someone can know for certain that Cicero will not make that choice and in the second that something of a certain kind causally necessitates Cicero's not making that choice. In my view the second statement suggests a more promising approach than the first to saying what "Cicero can choose to kill Caesar" means because it does not contain another "can" in the analysans and because it rests on the familiar view that a possible event is one whose nonoccurrence is not necessitated.

In taking this approach, I have been influenced by something that the philosopher A. C. Garnett once said when persuading Moore to alter his definition of a voluntary action as a preventable or avoidable action by adding the statement "Cicero could have chosen not to have killed Caesar" to "If Cicero had chosen not to have killed Caesar, Cicero would not have killed Caesar".[4] Garnett persuaded Moore to make this addition by convincing him that Cicero's killing of Caesar could not have been avoidable by Cicero if Cicero could not have chosen not to have killed Caesar; in such a case it would be false to say that Cicero could have avoided killing Caesar. Garnett held that a statement such as "Cicero could not have chosen not to have killed Caesar" would be supported, for example, by the statement "Cicero was having an attack of epileptic au-

[4] A. C. Garnett, "Moore's Theory of Moral Freedom and Responsibility", in *The Philosophy of G. E. Moore*, esp. pp. 179–80; also G. E. Moore, "A Reply to My Critics", ibid., pp. 623–24.

tomatism and *that* necessitated his not choosing to kill Caesar", which is equivalent to "Since Cicero was having an attack of epileptic automatism, he did not choose to kill Caesar". But this statement is only one of many statements of causal necessitation that might be said to support the statement "Cicero *could not have* chosen not to have killed Caesar", and therefore its denial is only one of many denials of causal necessitation that might be said to support "Cicero *could have* chosen not to have killed Caesar". Although Garnett presents only one sufficient condition for the truth of this statement, what he says leads me to think that a statement about the possibility of a choice is synonymous with a statement which denies that the agent's not making that choice is causally necessitated by a certain event or kind of event.

The unsatisfactory view that the denial of the statement "Since Cicero was having an attack of epileptic automatism, he did not choose not to kill Caesar" constitutes the analysis of "Cicero could not have chosen not to have killed Caesar", would be a satisfactory view if and only if a person's not choosing not to do something were always and only causally necessitated by that person's having an attack of epileptic automatism. But, of course, we might also say "Cicero could not have chosen not to kill Caesar" on the ground that his not choosing not to kill Caesar was necessitated by his being drugged, or by his having been hypnotized. Consequently, the affirmative statement "Cicero could have chosen not to have killed Caesar" is not synonymous with the denial of any *one* of these assertions of necessitation. Something similar is true of "Cicero could have chosen to kill Caesar" and of "Cicero can choose to kill Caesar".

If we believe, as I do, that "Cicero can choose to kill Caesar" need not and should not be regarded as synonymous with the statement, "Cicero's not choosing to kill Caesar is not causally necessitated by any event", we may say that it should be regarded as synonymous with an expression of the form "Cicero's not choosing to kill Caesar is not causally necessitated by the fact that Cicero is _____", where the blank is to be filled by an expression that results in a true statement. If, when we try to fill the blank so as to make a true statement, we conclude that none of the expressions, "having an attack of epileptic automatism", "drugged", or "hypnotized", yields a true statement which is synonymous with "Cicero can choose to kill Caesar", we may try to arrive at a sentence which *is* synonymous with that sentence by filling the blank with the alternation of these three expressions, namely, "having an attack of epileptic automatism, or drugged, or hypnotized". But then we may wonder whether filling the blank with this alternation is just as inadequate for arriving at a synonym as filling it with only one of the three alternants because we may wonder whether we have left out some other alternants, that is to say, expressions with as much claim to being in the alternation as the three that we have included in our analysis.

In order to deal with this problem, let us, for the sake of convenience, call these three causal necessitators of Cicero's nonchoice "appropriate precluders of Cicero's choice" and then try to say what an appropriate precluder of choice is. If we accept the principle that every obligatory choice is free (i.e., possible), I think we may say that an appropriate precluder is, like each of the three expressions above, a precluder of choice which, when it operates on an agent, removes the agent's duty to make that choice. So, if it is true that an appropriate precluder necessitates Cicero's not choosing to kill Caesar, then we may say that Cicero cannot choose to kill Caesar in an appropriate sense of "cannot". And if we are able to say truly that a given list of precluders of Cicero's choice is exhaustive—that they and only they are appropriate precluders—then, as we have seen, we may say that "Cicero cannot choose to kill Caesar" is synonymous with the statement that at least one of these listed precluders causally necessitates Cicero's not choosing to kill Caesar. In that case, of course, "Cicero can choose to kill Caesar" would be synonymous with the statement that none of the three mentioned appropriate precluders necessitates Cicero's not choosing to kill Caesar.

Notice, however, that the appropriate meaning of "can" is here tied to the three mentioned precluders, so we must be sure that they and they only make up the list. If they do, then "Cicero can choose to kill Caesar" is synonymous with "Cicero's not choosing to kill Caesar is not causally necessitated by Cicero's having an attack of epileptic automatism, nor by Cicero's being drugged, nor by Cicero's being hypnotized"; the definition of the expression "appropriate precluder" would be as follows: An appropriate precluder is identical with suffering an attack of epileptic automatism, or with being drugged, or with being hypnotized. Such an approach resembles Aristotle's in the *Nicomachean Ethics*, where he says that an involuntary action is one that is done in ignorance or under compulsion, and therefore holds that a voluntary action is one that is done neither in ignorance nor under compulsion.

The task of constructing a complete and exhaustive list of appropriate precluders would of course be made easier if we could answer the question "What is an appropriate precluder?" by stating a characteristic that all and only such precluders have. For if we could, we could analyze "Cicero can choose to kill Caesar" by saying "Cicero's not choosing to kill Caesar is not necessitated by any event which is an appropriate precluder of choice". Presenting this analysis of the notion of an appropriate precluder would obviate the need to present a list, remove our concern as to whether our list is exhaustive, and yield an analysis that would contrast neatly with the shorter analysis of the antideterminist who says that "Cicero can choose to kill Caesar" is synonymous with "Cicero's not choosing to kill Caesar is not necessitated by any event". The antideterminist's view implies that Cicero's not choosing to kill Caesar is not causally necessitated by *any* event whereas the philosopher who, for whatever reason, does not want to deny determinism will say that Cicero's not choosing to kill Caesar is not necessitated by any event that is of a certain specified kind.

If we do not specify this kind and adopt the listing approach instead, we should bear in mind that a statement of preclusion like "Cicero's choosing to kill Caesar is precluded by the fact that an ancestor of Cicero who lived before he was born once blinked his left eye", will probably be false—though one cannot be sure, of course—whatever names we put for "Cicero" and "Caesar". Therefore, the denial of such a statement of preclusion of choice will always be true and we would not list Cicero's ancestor's blinking of his left eye when trying to say what statement of preclusion of choice contradicts "Cicero can choose to kill Caesar". To say that Cicero's not choosing to kill Caesar is not causally necessitated by Cicero's ancestor's having blinked his left eye goes without saying, and that is why we are not likely to say it. By contrast, we would be likely to assert that some persons who fear to choose to perform an act of killing will, as a result, *not* choose to perform such an act, whereas others who have this fear overcome their fear and do choose to perform it. Blinking the left eye never precludes choice, we might say, whereas experiencing fear sometimes does and sometimes does not. The question, then, is whether "experiencing fear" should be on a list that also includes "suffering an attack of a choice-preventing disease", "hypnotized", and "drugged", each of which always precludes choice.

When I speak here of fear, I mean fear, for example, of sticking a dagger into the bloody body of another person who has already been stabbed by others. Let us suppose that Cicero does not make this choice because he is frightened in this way and his fear of making this choice causally precludes his making this choice. Such fear may be contrasted with Cicero's suffering an attack of a choice-preventing disease since the latter may be called an absolute or unconditional precluder of choice because it *of itself* precludes choice on the part of the agent. The same, I think, might be said of Cicero's having been appropriately drugged and also of his having been hypnotized into not choosing. All three of these precluders of Cicero's choice seem to be different in an important way from his fear of choosing to kill Caesar. This difference is reflected in the fact that the singular statement "Cicero's having suffered an attack of epileptic automatism causally necessitated his not choosing to kill Caesar" is supported by the law "No person who is having an attack of epileptic automatism will make choices", whereas "Cicero's fear of choosing to kill Caesar causally necessitates his not choosing to kill Caesar" is not supported by the law "No person who fears to make a choice will make that choice" since there is no such law. An absolute precluder such as having an attack of epileptic automatism will unconditionally, or of itself, preclude any human choice whereas fear of making a choice will be one of several conditions that jointly necessitate not making that choice. The person whose choice is precluded by fear will have other characteristics that join with his fear in necessitating his not choosing. They will appear in a generalization of the form: "Every person who is P, Q, and R, and who fears choosing to perform act A, will not choose to perform act A", which may be contrasted with "Every person who suffers an attack of epileptic automatism will not choose to perform act A", a statement which, I assume, is true as it stands.

I would add here that if fear of choosing to stick a dagger into the body of a person is not an absolute precluder of choice, then the fear of threatened pain or death is not for similar reasons. Suppose a person is told by a mugger that he will be killed if he chooses not to hand over his wallet. It may be said that his being threatened causally necessitates his *not* choosing *not* to hand over the wallet, and therefore precludes his choosing not to hand it over. He fears being killed, so he does not make a choice that he believes will get him killed. By contrast, the causal route from an attack of epileptic automatism to not choosing to kill Caesar is, so to speak, shorter. The connection between the mugger's threat and the victim's not choosing not to hand over the wallet is different from the connection between an attack of epileptic automatism and a person's not choosing not to kill, because there is no empirical law that will permit us to make an immediate causal inference from the mugger's threatening the victim to the victim's not choosing not to hand over the wallet. If only because some victims resist such threats, we must, when formulating the relevant law of behavior, add some attributes of the victim who does not resist. I know that other philosophers might distinguish the two examples by saying that when the victim hears the words "Your wallet or your life!", he chooses to save his life and therefore not to save his wallet, and that it is because he *can* make this choice that the connection here is different from the connection between an attack of a choice-preventing disease and a person's not choosing to kill Caesar. However, because I am using the concept of preclusion to analyze possible choice, I do not have the logical right, so to speak, to use such a concept of possible choice in characterizing the sense of "precludes" that I have in mind.

Before I proceed, I want to say (in a long parenthesis) that although I began this study by focusing on the problem posed by statements like "Cicero can kill Caesar", "Cicero could have killed Caesar", and "Cicero is free to kill Caesar", it should now be evident that the fundamental problem for me is not the problem of free *action* but rather the problem of free *choice*. In saying this, I do not wish to suggest that the problem of free action is of no interest. All I wish to note is the centrality of free choice in any discussion of free action that focuses as mine does on the contrast between different views of how to interpret the sentence "Cicero can choose to kill Caesar" with an eye, so to speak, on the impact that our interpretation will have on our belief in determinism.

I also want to offer the following additional considerations in favor of my interpretation of "Cicero can choose to kill Caesar". It has been argued that if, on a certain day, Cicero did not walk a mile in twenty minutes and did not walk a mile in four minutes, then determinism, which implies that whatever is the case must be the case, implies that on that day Cicero could not have walked a mile in twenty minutes and could not have walked a mile in four minutes. Therefore, if one accepts determinism yet wishes to say that on that day Cicero could have walked a mile in twenty minutes but could not have walked a mile in four minutes, one must use the word "could" in a sense different from that in which the determinist uses it when he says that Cicero could not have walked a twenty-minute mile or a four-minute mile that day. Accordingly, it has been said that this sense of "could" is expressed by the conditional statement "If Cicero had chosen to walk a mile in twenty minutes that day, he would have done so", which is supposed to be true, and by the conditional statement "If Cicero had chosen to walk a mile in four minutes that day, he would have done so", which is supposed to be false.

This conditionalist interpretation, as it has been called, is one that I think must be amended so as to add the statement "Cicero could have chosen to walk a mile in twenty minutes that day" to the first conditional statement above. But in that case, as we have seen, the question arises as to how this added statement should be interpreted. Suppose we begin, as we did in the case of Cicero's not walking, by assuming that Cicero did not choose to walk a mile in twenty minutes on the day in question and that he did not choose to walk a mile in four minutes. Then determinism presumably implies that Cicero could not have made either of these choices. But suppose we want to say in addition that Cicero could have made the first choice but not the second. How should we interpret this statement that we want to make? We have seen earlier that the conditionalist's interpretation of this statement is not defensible. What, then, should we say? Should we interpret "Cicero could have chosen to walk a twenty-minute mile but could not have chosen to walk a four-minute mile that day" as being synonymous with "Nothing causally necessitated Cicero's not choosing to walk a twenty-minute mile that day but something causally necessitated his not choosing to walk a four-minute mile that day"? If we do, we will, in the first part of this conjunctive statement, contradict our assumption that determinism is true. What, then, is left to us to say? In my opinion, we may say that a specific event, such as Cicero's having been hypnotized, causally necessitated his not choosing to walk a twenty-minute mile that day whereas such a specific event did not causally necessitate his not choosing to walk a four-minute mile. This allows us to say truthfully "Cicero could not have chosen to walk a mile in twenty minutes that day but could have chosen to walk a mile in four minutes" while admitting that a determinist might say truthfully "Cicero could not have chosen to walk a mile in twenty minutes that day and he could not have chosen to walk a mile in four minutes" simply because Cicero has made neither of these choices. We accomplished our goal by saying that a specific event did not preclude one choice whereas it did preclude the other. But, as we have seen, we may also accomplish it by saying that a specific kind of event did not preclude one choice whereas it did not preclude the other.

3. A Moral Belief Determines What an Appropriate Precluder Is, and This Moral Belief May Vary from Person to Person

If we say that fear of making a choice is not an absolute precluder of choice whereas an attack of a choice-precluding disease is, we might argue that there is an objective difference between the precluder fear and an absolute precluder such as an attack of epileptic automatism, but the question that is difficult to answer is this: Why should we say that an absolute precluder is the correct kind of precluder to refer to when formulating our analysis of "Cicero can choose to kill Caesar"? In other words, why should we identify the appropriateness of the precluder with its absoluteness as defined earlier? It might be replied that an absolute precluder is the only kind of precluder that all persons would fix on as the sort of precluder whose absence determines the meaning of a sentence such as "Cicero can choose to kill Caesar". But I doubt this because I doubt that this sentence's so-called "real meaning" is presented by analyzing it as synonymous with "It is false that Cicero's not choosing to kill Caesar is causally necessitated by an event that absolutely precludes his choosing to kill Caesar". I believe that someone who wished to include fear as an appropriate precluder even though it was not absolute might understandably insist that those who use absolute preclusion as a criterion do so for no good reason. But how do we resolve the dispute between such a person and someone who insists on limiting the class of appropriate precluders to those that are absolute? In my opinion we cannot resolve this dispute by appealing to some "real meaning" of the expression "can choose" or of the expression "free choice" which we must analyze in exactly one way.

I am therefore led to a form of relativism or pluralism that links the selection of appropriate precluders of choice with one's own moral view as to whether a precluder is an obligation-removing precluder. A precluder will be appropriate if it removes the agent's duty to perform the action under consideration. Suppose it is true that if Cicero chooses to kill Caesar, he will kill him. And suppose that his choice is precluded by his fear of making that choice. If one person believes that Cicero's presumed duty to kill Caesar has been removed because his choice has been precluded by fear, then that person will regard fear as an appropriate precluder. But if another person does not believe this, then this other person will not regard fear as an appropriate precluder. The important question is whether

47

this other person accepts the moral statement that fear serves as an excuse for not doing what would otherwise be obligatory. If he does, then he will reject the view that only absolute precluders of choice are excusatory. But I see no way of talking him out of rejecting this view without showing him that he is making a moral mistake, and showing him this will be extremely difficult or impossible. Only a philosopher who thinks he can show that it is morally wrong for anyone to regard fear as an appropriate precluder would seem to be in a position to criticize those who regard it as appropriate. We can see how difficult it is to fix on a characteristic such as absoluteness as a criterion of appropriate precluders when we reflect that an absolute precluder of choice that has been instituted by the agent himself may not be regarded as an appropriate precluder. I mean, for example, that if a man drugs himself with the intention of avoiding his duty to make a choice, we may deny (though we need not) that his being drugged is an excuse for his not choosing to do his duty.[5]

Alternatively, a philosopher might offer a criterion that differs from that of absolute preclusion; he might substi-

---

[5] See W. Sinnott-Armstrong, "'Ought' Conversationally Implies 'Can'", *Philosophical Review* 93 (1984): 251–54, where it is argued that "if ought entailed can , an agent could escape having to do something simply by making himself unable to do it". This is illustrated by a case in which the agent makes himself unable to keep a promise to meet a person at a certain place at a certain time by deliberately seeing to it that it is physically impossible for the agent to meet him at that place at that time. Similarly, from my point of view, Cicero would make himself unable to perform the obligatory act of killing Caesar by arranging things so that it would be false to say "If Cicero were to choose to kill Caesar, he would kill him". Cicero, for example, might see to it that he was tied in such a way as to prevent this conditional statement from being true.

However, I am at this point calling attention to a different sort of case in which Cicero drugs himself so that he cannot choose to kill Caesar and thereby tries to evade his obligation to kill him. According to my view, Cicero's drugging himself in an effort to be absolutely precluded from

tute the notion of a precluder which is external to the agent's mind for that of an absolute precluder of choice. But this criterion of externality is likely to be unsatisfactory, not only because of the difficulty of knowing what is in the mind and out of it but also because not all the precluders that one might regard as appropriate would be regarded as external to the agent's mind even if one did have a criterion for being external. I can see why a hypnotic trance might be said to be brought about by something external to the agent's mind and I can also see why his being in a drugged state might be said to be caused by something external to his mind. But if an attack of epileptic automatism is an appropriate precluder, then it would seem that not all appropriate precluders of choice are external to the agent's mind. The idea that appropriate precluders of choice are appropriate just in case they are external may be modeled on the idea that precluded physical actions are said to be precluded by external factors, as when a man fails to walk more than a few feet from a certain spot because he is chained to that spot. This man's walking more than a few feet may be said to be precluded by something external to him and he may for this reason be excused for not walking more than a few feet if, for some reason, he had promised to do so and had thereby incurred an obligation to do so. However, the preclusion of choice seems to be different. If choice is said to occur in the mind, it would seem that another mental event, such as an attack of epileptic automatism, might preclude choice.

In saying, however, that absoluteness may be preferred to externality as a criterion for being an appropriate pre-

choosing to kill Caesar would not create an excuse for his not performing an action that is regarded as obligatory unless Cicero can morally justify his drugging of himself.

cluder, I do not say that it ought to be preferred by everyone. That is why I do not think that a moralist who excuses an agent for not doing his duty on the ground that his choosing to do his duty was precluded by fear must accept the criterion of absoluteness. He may object that *he* believes that a person's fearing to choose to plunge a dagger into a body made bloody by the daggers of others is a ground for excusing that person for not doing his duty. But how can we show that the objector is wrong to think so, even if it is true that most of his countrymen accept the criterion of absoluteness that excludes fear from the class of precluders? Because I do not know how to show this in a more direct way by focusing on the words "cannot choose", I say that when a philosopher decides which precluders of choice are appropriate, he will be guided by his own moral belief as to which listed precluders, or what specified kind of precluder, will excuse an agent from making a certain choice and therefore from performing a certain action. Later we will see how this plays a part in the holistic comparison of rival theories about free will.

4. The Argument up to Now

Before I try to say something further in the next chapter about some of the logical and semantic ideas used in this one, I want to remind the reader of how I have arrived at this point in my argument. I began with the idea that "Cicero can kill Caesar" is not fully analyzed by "If Cicero chooses to kill Caesar, he will kill him" because we must add "Cicero can choose to kill Caesar". Then I expressed disagreement with a number of views as to how we should interpret this last statement, especially with the view that a possible choice is one that is causally necessitated by nothing. One of my main points in this chapter is that a statement such as "Cicero can choose to kill Caesar" need not be interpreted in this way because, when it is construed as saying what "Cicero's not choosing to kill Caesar is not necessitated" says elliptically, the ellipsis need not be completed by adding the phrase "by any other event". It may be completed by adding various other expressions. I have also said that the decision of a person to complete the ellipsis in a different way depends on that person's moral belief as to what precluders of a choice remove an agent's obligation to make that choice. For when we say that a precluder of such a choice removes a certain obligation we are making use of the moral principle, "A choice is obligatory only if the agent can make it", a principle that may mean different things to different persons because their moral attitudes and beliefs lead them to accept different interpretations of the phrase "can make the choice".[6] However, I should say here that I do not regard

[6] I have been defending the view that the principle linking "ought" and "can", or "ought" and "free" is a moral principle for more than thirty years, but in my earlier writings on the subject I failed to formulate the principle in what I now regard as a satisfactory way. See my review of Isaiah Berlin's *Historical Inevitability*, which originally appeared in *Perspectives USA* 16 (Summer 1956), pp. 191–96, reprinted in my *Religion, Politics, and the Higher Learning* (Cambridge, Mass.: Harvard University Press, 1959), esp. pp. 78–84; also my paper "Moral Judgment and Voluntary Action", in the *Harry Austryn Wolfson Jubilee Volume, English Section* (Jerusalem: American Academy for Jewish Research, 1965), Vol. 2, pp. 819–31, reprinted with some alterations in my *Foundations of Historical Knowledge* (New York, 1965), pp. 271–91. Berlin has replied to my criticism of his views; see his *Four Essays on Liberty*, (Oxford: Oxford University Press, 1969), pp. xix–xxiii, xxxvi–xxxvii. Also see my rejoinder, "Oughts and Cans" in *The Idea of Freedom: Essays in Honour of Isaiah Berlin*, ed. A. Ryan (Oxford: Oxford University Press, 1979), pp. 211–19.

For an illuminating discussion of the principle linking "ought" and "can" which lends some support to the view that the principle is a moral one, see Jaakko Hintikka, "Some Main Problems of Deontic Logic", in *Deontic Logic* ed. R. Hilpinen (Dordrecht: Reidel, 1970), pp. 59–104, to

the notion of appropriate precluder as itself a moral notion for reasons that I will discuss later. I should also say
that my assertion that we need not say that a possible
choice is one that is causally necessitated by nothing is
different from my assertion that an alternative view is preferable. The latter assertion will also be discussed later,
when I compare different theories in a holistic or corporatist way.

which Dagfinn Follesdal has kindly called my attention. I want to say,
however, that Hintikka's interpretation of the principle differs from mine
insofar as his interpretation seems to make the principle more truistic, so
to speak, than I think it is.

Expansion, Analysis, and
Free Choice

IN THIS CHAPTER I want to probe more deeply into some of the philosophical ideas that I have previously used; for example, the idea of an elliptical sentence, the idea of expanding such a sentence, and the idea of analyzing the sentence into which it is expanded. Much of what I have said so far depends on regarding the sentence "Cicero's not choosing to kill Caesar is not causally necessitated" as elliptical or incomplete because it invites the question "By what?" just as the sentence "Caligula is not loved" invites the question "By whom?". Therefore, the sentence about Cicero must be expanded or completed if one is to express what it means in a complete way, and after that the complete sentence may be analyzed. While incomplete it resembles in a certain respect the incomplete arithmetical expression "5 is not greater". One may imagine that this arithmetical expression has been uttered in the midst of an exchange in which the speaker is understood by an interlocutor despite the incompleteness of the speaker's utterance. Both of them agree that it should be expanded, for example, into "5 is not greater than 6" or "5 is not greater than any number between 6 and 12", depending on what the speaker has in mind. After that, the statement containing "not greater than" may be analyzed, just as the statement containing "not causally necessitated by" may be.

As we have seen, when a philosopher who tries to clarify "Cicero can choose to kill Caesar" replaces it by the elliptical sentence "Cicero's not choosing to kill Caesar is not causally necessitated", the philosopher, when asked "By what?", may, for example, reply: "By Cicero's having an attack of a choice-preventing disease"; or "By Cicero's having an attack of epileptic automatism, by his being drugged, or by his being hypnotized"; or "By something that absolutely precludes choice"; or "By any other event". Any one of these completions will make sense in the context, and that is why we are not required to add "by any other event" as if only the result of that completion expressed the meaning which the elliptical sentence incompletely expresses. Indeed, I believe that one of the other sorts of completions is to be preferred when we take into account the whole body of statements—the Duhemian conjunction or theory—that will contain the expansion of the incomplete sentence uttered by the speaker; but I freely grant that a rival antideterministic completion might appear in a theory preferred by someone else, as we shall see later. Because I believe we need to say more about rival bodies of statements, I later take up the question whether a body containing a completion of "Cicero's not choosing to kill Caesar is not necessitated" which adds "by anything" constitutes a theory that is inferior to one that adds "by", followed by a reference to something more specific. Before I do that, however, I want to say something further about the semantical and logical underpinnings of viewing "Cicero can choose to kill Caesar" as a sentence that may be replaced by the elliptical sentence "Cicero's not choosing to kill Caesar is not causally necessitated", which may then be expanded into different statements.

1. Expanding and Analyzing
"Cicero Can Choose to Kill
Caesar"

A convenient way to understand "Cicero can choose to kill Caesar" is to think of it as the denial of "Cicero cannot choose to kill Caesar" and to note that the latter sentence, when used in discussions of free will, does not deny the logical possibility of Cicero's choosing to kill Caesar but rather its natural possibility. When denying the logical possibility of, say, Cicero's being a man and not an animal, we do not speak elliptically since the sentence "It is not logically possible that Cicero is a man and not an animal" is a complete sentence and may be analyzed as meaning the same as "It is logically necessary that if Cicero is a man, then he is an animal". But when we deny the natural possibility of Cicero's choosing to kill Caesar we often speak elliptically insofar as we mean to say, but fall short of saying, for example, either (1) that Cicero's choosing to kill Caesar is naturally impossible relative to some specific event pertaining to Cicero such as his having an attack of epileptic automatism; or (2) that Cicero's choosing to kill Caesar is naturally impossible relative to some event pertaining to Cicero which absolutely precludes his making a choice. The completion in case (1) is analogous in a certain respect to completing the sentence "5 is not greater" by adding the words "than 6" whereas the completion in case (2) is analogous in a certain respect to completing it by adding the words "than any number between 6 and 12". We can more specifically indicate the two kinds of relativity I have mentioned by saying in case (1) that the combination of Cicero's choosing to kill Caesar and Cicero's having an attack of epileptic automatism is naturally impossible, or by saying in case (2) that there is an event pertaining to Cicero which absolutely precludes choice and which is such that the combination of it and Cicero's choosing to kill Caesar is naturally impossible.

In the light of this, we may say that "Cicero can choose to kill Caesar" means what is expressed by the denial of what we assert in case (1) or by the denial of what we assert in case (2). That is, it may mean the same as "It is not naturally impossible that Cicero has an attack of epileptic automatism and that he chooses to kill Caesar"; or it may mean the same as "It is false that there is an event pertaining to Cicero which absolutely precludes choice and which is such that the conjunction of it and Cicero's choosing to kill Caesar is naturally impossible". In addition, we may provide for the case where Cicero's choosing to kill Caesar is said to be naturally impossible relative to Cicero's having an attack of epileptic automatism, or his being drugged, or his being hypnotized, by regarding this as an example of case (1) and saying "It is not naturally impossible that Cicero chooses to kill Caesar and that Cicero has the property of having an attack of epileptic automatism or of being drugged or of being hypnotized". Case (1) represents what I earlier called the listing approach, where the list may consist of one item, as when we list only Cicero's having an attack of epileptic automatism, or where it may consist of several items, as when we list as alternants his having such an attack, his being drugged, and his being hypnotized.

It may be helpful to add that we have in case (1) expanded "Cicero cannot choose to kill Caesar"—which we may first conveniently transform into "~Naturally possible (Cicero chooses to kill Caesar)" by using parentheses in familiar logical fashion and the tilde as a sign of negation—

into "Cicero is having an attack of epileptic automatism and ~naturally possible (Cicero is having an attack of epileptic automatism and Cicero chooses to kill Caesar)". And after having expanded it into this conjunction, we may analyze what this conjunction means. By applying certain familiar laws of logical equivalence to the second conjunct we may transform the whole conjunction into the following conjunction: "Cicero is having an attack of epileptic automatism, and naturally necessary (if Cicero is having an attack of epileptic automatism, then ~Cicero chooses to kill Caesar)". It follows that the elliptical sentence "Cicero can choose to kill Caesar" may be expanded and then analyzed so that it means the same as the denial of the conjunction that expresses what "Cicero cannot choose to kill Caesar" means, namely, the alternation: "Either Cicero is not having an attack of epileptic automatism or it is not naturally necessary that if Cicero is having an attack of epileptic automatism, then ~Cicero chooses to kill Caesar".[1]

In case (2) we expand "Cicero cannot choose to kill Caesar" and therefore "~Naturally possible (Cicero chooses to kill Caesar)", into "There is a C such that C absolutely precludes choice and ~naturally possible (Cicero is C and Cicero chooses to kill Caesar)". This in turn is equivalent to "There is a C such that C absolutely precludes choice and naturally necessary (if Cicero is C, then ~Cicero chooses to kill Caesar)". Therefore, in case (2) the denial of this last

[1] I am grateful to Saul Kripke for helping me clarify my views on this. Recall that "Brutus can choose to kill Caesar" is supposed to be true and also synonymous with the denial of the factual conditional statement "Since Brutus is having an attack of epileptic automatism, Brutus does not choose to kill Caesar". This statement implies that Brutus is having an attack of epileptic automatism. In that case, denying the factual conditional statement is equivalent to denying its antecedent or the statement that this antecedent causally implies its consequent.

existential statement is the analyzed expansion of "Cicero can choose to kill Caesar". It is equivalent to affirming that nothing which absolutely precludes choice and which pertains to Cicero causally necessitates Cicero's not choosing to kill Caesar. We have seen earlier that it is extremely important for a philosopher who does not wish to deny determinism to include the restrictive condition that C absolutely precludes choice—or some similar condition—so that he does not expand and then analyze "Cicero can choose to kill Caesar" in a manner that makes it synonymous with the antideterministic statement, "Nothing causally necessitates Cicero's not choosing to kill Caesar".

Once we see that "Possible (Cicero chooses to kill Caesar)" may be transformed by expansion and analysis in either of these two ways, we can see that important philosophical questions remain after we have decided about the way to transform it. If we transform it in the manner of (1), we may be asked whether there is one and only one precluding characteristic of Cicero that all persons are bound to mention when correctly transforming "Cicero cannot choose to kill Caesar". And if we transform it in the manner of (2), we may be asked whether all persons are bound to characterize the existent precluder of choice as, for example, absolute in the sense earlier defined.

In addition I have argued that while trying to answer the second question, we should always keep in mind that a precluder of Cicero's choice which renders Cicero not free to kill Caesar is one that renders Cicero's killing of Caesar not obligatory if we accept the moral principle which says that we have an obligation or duty to do only what we are free to do as well as an analysis of "Cicero can kill Caesar" that implies "Cicero can choose to kill Caesar". Accepting this moral principle and this sort of analysis, I have said that we may identify a choice-precluding event as appropriate if and only if it makes Cicero's killing of Caesar and his choosing to kill him nonobligatory. Therefore, if we want to test whether Cicero's fear of killing Caesar is an appropriate precluder, we may ask whether the statement that it precludes Cicero's choosing to kill Caesar *morally* implies that Cicero is not obligated to kill him. This means that we must find out whether the statement that Cicero is not obligated to kill Caesar is supported by a moral argument which contains as one of its descriptive premises the statement that Cicero was on a given occasion afraid to choose to kill Caesar. And we will say that this episode of fear is not an appropriate precluder if we do not think that Cicero's not choosing to kill Caesar out of fear is a basis for denying that he has an obligation to kill Caesar.

This shows that we may determine whether a precluder of choice is an appropriate precluder in case (1) by asking ourselves the moral question: Does this precluder of choice excuse, that is to say remove, the agent's obligation to perform the act? Here, one man's excuse may not be another's. Something similar is true in case (2). One person may think that only an absolute precluder removes an obligation whereas another person may not think so. That is why I am not inclined to defend the idea that there is exactly one universally acceptable characterization of precluders of choice that makes them obligation-removers. In other words, I find it hard to defend the idea that after "Cicero can choose to kill Caesar" has been transformed by way of expansion and analysis into a sentence of the form, "Cicero's choosing to kill Caesar is not precluded by the fact that Cicero is C", the variable "C" must be replaced in the same way by all persons. I also find it hard to defend the idea that all persons must put the same predicate for the variable "K" after transforming "Cicero cannot choose to kill Caesar" into "There is at least one event C of kind *K* such that Cicero is *C* and such that it is naturally necessary that if Cicero is *C*, then Cicero does not choose to kill Caesar". That is why it is extremely difficult to say which of the many senses of "can" that might be licensed by method (1) or method (2) is the sense of "can" used when we say "Cicero can choose to kill Caesar". Different persons who hold different moral views may regard different events as appropriate precluders whether they adopt method (1) or method (2) of interpreting "Cicero can choose to kill Caesar". Consequently, if one changes one's criterion for being an obligation-removing precluder of choice, one changes what one means by the statement that an obligatory action is a free action because one changes one's meaning of "free". Moreover, different societies, and different individuals in a given society, may differ about the meaning of "free" because they do not regard the same precluders of choice as obligation-removers. Some will be more lenient than others when it comes to saying that a certain precluder or a certain kind of precluder removes obligation—lenient because, for example, they regard fear as such a precluder when others do not.

If I am right, therefore, transforming "Cicero can choose to kill Caesar" into the statement that nothing causes Cicero not to choose to kill Caesar is not logically required because one may complete the elliptical sentence "Cicero's not choosing to kill Caesar is not necessitated" in other ways, depending on one's other views. The completion which consists in adding to "Cicero's not choosing to kill Caesar is not necessitated" the phrase "by anything" is not the only acceptable completion. This lends further support to my idea, set forth in an earlier chapter, that the conjunction "Cicero ought to kill Caesar and Cicero cannot choose to kill Caesar" is not self-contradictory and not nonsensical. Rather it is a meaningful sentence that may be uttered by someone who does not accept the moral principle that every obligatory action is one that the agent can choose to perform. Later, when I try to show why the sorts of completions or expansions that I favor are preferable by viewing them as components of conjunctive philosophical theories that are evaluated in a holistic or corporatist manner, I stress the interdependence of one's view of how to complete such a sentence and one's view of the meaning of the statement that an act is obligatory only if it is free.

This, however, is a convenient place at which to ward off a misunderstanding. I do not claim that freedom of choice is a moral concept. And, I repeat, I do not say that "S is morally obligated to do A" logically implies "S is free to do A". I have indicated that I regard the latter sentence as replaceable by a four-part conjunction that contains two conditional conjuncts; namely, "If S chooses to do A, then S does A" and "If S chooses not to do A, then S does not do A". Since these two conditional conjuncts will always be descriptive, the four-part conjunction will be moral or nondescriptive only if the two remaining conjuncts, "S can choose to do A" and "S can choose not to do A", are moral; and I deny that they are for reasons that I want to spell out.

Every completion or expansion of the elliptical sentence "S's not choosing to do A is not causally necessitated" that I consider while offering an interpretation of "S can choose to do A" is a descriptive statement. Thus I have considered illustrations in which S's not choosing to do A is not causally necessitated by an attack of a mental disease or by S's having been hypnotized; the same would be true of illustrations that I might offer as expansions of "S can choose not to do A". The only reason why a reader might think that I regard the concept of free or possible choice as a moral concept is that I have said that we may determine what expansions are correct by asking whether our filling the blank in "S's not choosing to do A is not causally necessitated by S's being _____" yields a statement which is morally implied—in a sense I have earlier specified—by "S has a moral obligation to choose to do A". But it should not be concluded from this that I regard free choice as a moral concept, or that I regard a statement produced by filling the blank as a moral statement. I have said only that we may *test* the correctness of our descriptive blank-filling by seeing whether that blank-filling results in a statement that is morally implied by "S has a moral obligation to choose to do A"; this does *not* turn a statement which meets that test into a moral statement. It follows that all four conjuncts in my proposed analysis of "S is free to do A" will be descriptive and nonmoral. It also follows that this descriptive, nonmoral statement is not logically implied by "S has a moral obligation to choose to do A".

Perhaps it would help if I were to point out that a moralist might also test the correctness of definitions of descriptive terms such as "lying" and "stealing" by seeing whether those definitions preserve the truth of moral statements such as "No one ought to lie" and "No one ought to steal". A moralist might well reject a definition of "lie" because it did not preserve the truth of "No one ought to lie". It might also help if I were to point out that my approach to the elliptical "Possible (Cicero chooses to kill Caesar)" is guided by the logical idea that it is equivalent to the equally elliptical "Cicero's not choosing to kill Caesar is not causally necessitated". But when I test the expansion of the latter into "Cicero's not choosing to kill Caesar is not causally necessitated by Cicero's having an attack of epileptic automatism", I appeal beyond logic to the moral principle that every obligatory choice is a possible choice in order to see whether this expansion is acceptable to me.

2. What Is an Appropriate Conditional Statement in the Analysis of "Cicero Can Kill Caesar"?

The idea that we may test the appropriateness of a precluder of choice by asking and answering a moral question finds a parallel in our reflection on the appropriateness of the conditional conjuncts in a full analysis of "Cicero is free to kill Caesar" that reads: "If Cicero chooses to kill Caesar, he will kill him; if he chooses not to kill him, he will not kill him; he can choose to kill him; and he can choose not to kill him". We have concentrated on the third conjunct, but suppose we are asked why we include the first and second conditional conjuncts in our definiens or analysans. In my view, we should reject any replacements for the first and second conjuncts that contain antecedents which do not preserve the truth of the moral statement that "Ought" implies "Can". The selection that takes place when we decide which precluders are appropriate finds a counterpart in our decision that "choose" and "choose not" should be used as the dominant verbs in the antecedents of the two conditional statements appearing in the definition of free action. But just as there is more than one precluder of choice that, when it pertains to Cicero, permits us to say that Cicero cannot choose to kill Caesar, so there are verbs other than "choose" that may appear as dominant verbs in the antecedents of the conditional statements that we use to express the idea that Cicero can kill Caesar. I mean, for example, that the sen-

tence "Cicero can kill Caesar" might be analyzed by someone as meaning the same as "If Cicero hopes to kill Caesar,
he will kill him; and Cicero can hope to kill Caesar" and yet
not be thought to express the sense of "can" that allows us
to say that if Cicero cannot kill Caesar, he has no duty to
kill him. My point is that we can express one sense of "can"
by using the verb "hope" in this way, but not a sense of
"can" which permits us to say that if Cicero ought to kill
Caesar, then he can. If one thinks that hoping never brings
about what is hoped for, one would of course not use
"hope" as the dominant verb in the antecedent of the
causal conditional statement that appears in our analysis
of "can". But if one thinks that hope is sometimes efficacious and sometimes not, one might say that "hope" has
something important in common with "choose", since
choosing to do something is sometimes efficacious and
sometimes not. Taking a cue from the term "water-solu-
ble", we may say that actions are hope-doable[2] just in case
we *can* hope to do them and by hoping to do them, do
them, but add that hope-doability is not morally implied
by the obligatoriness of an action whereas choice-doabil-
ity *is* so morally implied. The verb "pray" is similar to
"hope" in this respect. I (and many of my readers, I pre-
sume) would not say that if an action is not pray-doable,
it is not obligatory. And yet it might be said that a pray-
doable action is an action that one can do in one sense of
"can".

Of course, some persons might say that "Ought" implies
"Pray-doability". They might really think that a man who
failed to perform an action that he prayed to do would be
excused from an obligation to perform it. They might say:

[2] This term is constructed in imitation of the expression "water-solu-
ble" because, obviously, "hopable" does not do the job. "Hopable" is like
"choosable" and therefore not like "choice-doable".

"Poor man! Even prayer did not lead to his performing that action! So surely he has no duty to do what prayer could not bring about!". They might analyze "Mr. Hea can kill Caesar" as follows: "If Mr. Hea prays that he will kill Caesar, Mr. Hea will kill him; and Mr. Hea can pray that he will kill Caesar; and if Mr. Hea prays that he will not kill Caesar, Mr. Hea will not kill him; and Mr. Hea can pray that he will not kill Caesar". (How such people analyze "Mr. Hea can pray that he will kill Caesar" and "Mr. Hea can pray that he will not kill Caesar" is another matter.) What I want to emphasize is that such people would excuse Mr. Hea from doing his duty if the first or the second conditional statement in their analysis of "Mr. Hea can kill Caesar" were false. Therefore, they would disagree morally with anyone who denied that the falsity of this conditional excused Mr. Hea from doing his duty. That is why we must use appropriate antecedents in the conditional statements that we include in our analysis of "Mr. Hea is free to kill Caesar" just as we must use appropriate precluders in our analysis of "Mr. Hea is free to choose to kill Caesar". And in both cases appropriateness may be tested by appealing to a moral belief even though the statement "Mr. Hea is free to kill Caesar" does not itself express a moral belief. Later on, I shall try to say why the situation here is different from that in which we make purely physical "can"-statements like "This cube of sugar can dissolve in water". My main point here is that the verb in the antecedent of a conditional statement that appears in the analysis of "S can do A" will not be an acceptable component of that analysis if it does not preserve the truth, so to speak, of the principle that every obligatory action is one that can be performed.

"He Can Do It",
"He Will Do It if He Chooses",
"He Can Do It if He Chooses", and
"He Can Choose to Do It":
Some Views about
How They Are Related

SO FAR I have focused primarily on the sentence "Cicero can choose to kill Caesar" as a conjunct of my interpretation of "Cicero is free to kill Caesar". Although I will say something more here about this conjunct, I want to turn first to some important questions concerning the two conditional conjuncts in my interpretation, namely, "If Cicero chooses to kill Caesar, he will kill Caesar" and "If Cicero chooses not to kill Caesar, he will not kill him."

I believe with many philosophers that the first is a causal conditional statement that says that Cicero's choice will cause, bring about, or produce Cicero's action just as the striking of a match will cause it to light; I also believe something analogous about the second conditional statement. With this in mind, I want to deal here with a number of issues that have emerged in the writings of philosophers who have asked the following questions: (1) Is the first statement a causal conditional statement and does it, by itself, present the analysis of "Cicero can kill Caesar?" (2) How does it help to add "Cicero can choose to kill Caesar" to the analysis? (3) What is the relationship between the statement "If Cicero chooses to kill Caesar, he *will* kill him" and the statement "If Cicero chooses to kill Caesar, he *can* kill him"? (4) And what is the relationship between the statement "If Cicero had chosen to kill Caesar, he *would* have killed him" and the statement "If Cicero had chosen to kill Caesar, he *could* have killed him"?

1. "He Will if He Chooses" and "He Would Have if He Had Chosen" Are Causal Conditionals

Criticism has been directed against the view that statements such as "If Brutus chooses to kill Caesar, he will kill him" and "If Cicero had chosen to kill Caesar, he would have killed him" are both causal in just the sense in which the statements "If this match is struck, it will light" and "If that match had been struck, it would have lit" are causal.[1] When Moore illustrates this view in *Ethics* he has an unfortunate tendency to use first-person sentences such as "I should have run a mile in twenty minutes this morning if I had chosen", and I think that some criticism of Moore depends on excessive preoccupation with the peculiarities of this sort of illustration. Criticism has also been focused on Moore's equally unfortunate tendency to oscillate between saying that a sentence such as "Moore could have run a mile in twenty minutes this morning" is synonymous with "Moore could have run a mile in twenty minutes this morning if he had chosen to do so" and saying that it is

[1] Austin, *Philosophical Papers*, pp. 153–80. Also see my "Causation and Action", *Philosophy, Science, and Method: Essays in Honor of Ernest Nagel*, ed. S. Morgenbesser, P. Suppes, and M. White (New York: St. Martin's Press, 1969), pp. 251–53.

synonymous with "Moore *would* have run a mile in twenty minutes this morning *if* he had chosen to do so". Consequently, as we shall see, Moore would have fared much better at the hands of some critics if he had avoided the use of first-person illustrations in favor of third-person illustrations, and if he had made it quite clear that his thesis was that "Moore could have run a mile in twenty minutes this morning" is to be analyzed as meaning the same as "Moore *would* have run a mile in twenty minutes this morning if Moore had chosen to do so", and not to be analyzed as meaning the same as "Moore *could* have run a mile in twenty minutes this morning if Moore had chosen to do so".

I turn now to a criticism of the view that the first-person sentence "I could have run a mile in twenty minutes this morning" is to be analyzed as meaning the same as "I should have run a mile in twenty minutes this morning if I had chosen". It has been argued that the second statement is not a causal conditional statement, but sometimes such an argument has required irrelevant concentration on features that it has as a first-person sentence which its third-person counterpart does not have. Thus the sentence "I should have run a mile in twenty minutes this morning if I had chosen" has been called "an unusual, not to say queer, specimen of English";[2] and it has been said in a very British way that this sentence means the same as "If I had chosen to run a mile in twenty minutes this morning, I should (jolly well) have done so". One may agree with these observations but deny, as I do, that this sentence is an assertion by the speaker of the speaker's strength of character, or an assertion of the fact that he puts his decisions into execution.[3] But, more importantly, one may

---

[2] Austin, *Philosophical Papers*, p. 156.

[3] It seems to me that the sentence is not an assertion of the speaker's

correctly deny that an argument which shows that a first-person sentence does not mean something of the form "If I had made a certain choice, my making that choice would have caused me to do something",[4] shows that the third-person statement "He would have run a mile in twenty minutes if he had chosen" is not a causal statement.

There are other first-person conditional statements that one may rightly characterize as not being causal, but the fact that there are does not count against the view that their third-person counterparts are causal. Consider what has been said about the sentence "I shall (do it) if I choose (to do it)" in an effort to show that it is not causal. It has been contrasted with "I shall ruin him if I am extravagant" by pointing out that while the latter is causal, the former is not because it makes good sense to stress the "shall" in the former but not in the latter. But this difference disappears when we turn to third-person counterparts of these sentences, such as "He will do it if he chooses to do it" and "He (Smith) will ruin him (Jones) if he (Smith) is extravagant". Therefore, we cannot validly use the argument about stress in order to show that the former sentence is not causal by comparison with the latter; both are causal.

Had Moore used only third-person illustrations throughout his discussion of free will in *Ethics*—and he certainly could have while supporting his general view—he would

---

strength of character though it may be said to imply that the speaker's character is strong. Similarly, "If that match had been struck, it would have lit" does not assert that the match was dry; at best it implies that it was. In both of these cases it would seem even better to say that the contrary-to-fact conditional statement implies that there are statements which in conjunction with the antecedent of the conditional statement lead by law to the consequent, where these statements need not be implied by the conditional itself. This is more evident, perhaps, when we consider "He would have run a mile in twenty minutes if he had chosen".

[4] Austin, *Philosophical Papers*, p. 157.

have avoided the criticism that "I shall" in "I shall if I choose" is "not an assertion of *fact* but an expression of *intention*, verging towards the giving of some variety of undertaking".[5] Obviously, the sentence "He will run a mile in twenty minutes if he chooses" is not an expression of intention, and therefore the observation that "I shall if I choose" is one, even if correct, cuts no ice against the view that this third-person sentence is causal. It is worth emphasizing, moreover, that since Moore was mainly concerned in his *Ethics* with moral statements about actions, he could have confined himself to using third-person moral statements such as "Russell ought to have walked a mile in twenty minutes yesterday". In that case Moore might well have used the statement "If Russell had chosen not to walk a mile in twenty minutes yesterday, he would not have done so" when illustrating the sort of conditional statement that he thought would have to be true if one were properly to make an "ought"-statement about an action.

2. "He Could Have Walked if He Had Chosen" and "He Would Have Walked if He Had Chosen": Their Relations with Each Other and with "He Could Have Walked"

Now I turn to the polemical exploitation of the tendency of Moore and other philosophers to say that "Moore could have run a mile in twenty minutes this morning" is synonymous with "Moore could have run a mile in twenty minutes this morning if he had chosen to do so" and *also* syn-

[5] Ibid., p. 161.

onymous with "Moore *would* have run a mile in twenty
minutes this morning if Moore had chosen to do so". A
good deal of effort has been devoted to showing that
"Moore *could* have walked a mile in twenty minutes this
morning if he had chosen to do so" is *not* a causal conditional statement, but in my opinion this is irrelevant since
I do not think that Moore—when speaking in what he regarded as the most exact way—had to maintain that this
statement is a causal conditional statement. All he had to
do was to maintain that "Moore *would* have walked a mile
in twenty minutes this morning if he had chosen to do
so" is.

One criticism has it that the sentences "Moore could
have walked a mile in twenty minutes" and "Moore can
walk a mile in twenty minutes" are sometimes regarded by
Moore as elliptical, as incompletely expressing what would
be fully expressed by "Moore could have walked a mile in
twenty minutes if he had chosen to walk a mile in twenty
minutes" and by "Moore can walk a mile in twenty minutes if he chooses to walk a mile in twenty minutes" re-
spectively. Yet Moore also writes sometimes as though he
wants to analyze the sentence "Moore can walk a mile in
twenty minutes" as meaning the same as "Moore will walk
a mile in twenty minutes if he chooses"; and therefore, it
has been said, Moore confused expansion with analysis
when dealing with a sentence such as "Moore can walk
a mile in twenty minutes". It is difficult to say whether
Moore did confuse them, but I am not convinced that he
did even though he often says that "can"-sentences, "can
if"-sentences, and "will if"-sentences, as well as "could"-
sentences, "could if"-sentences, and "would if"-sentences
mean the same.[6] In support of the view that he was mainly

[6] Moore, *Ethics*, esp. pp. 10–12.

concerned to analyze "can"-sentences as synonymous with "will if"-sentences and "could"-sentences as synonymous with "would if"-sentences, I lean heavily on the last two sentences of the following passage in Moore's *Ethics*:

> What is the sense of the word 'could', in which it is so certain that we often *could* have done, what we did not do? What, for instance, is the sense in which I *could* have walked a mile in twenty minutes this morning, though I did not? There is one suggestion, which is very obvious: namely, that what I mean is simply after all that I could, *if* I had chosen; or (to avoid a possible complication) perhaps we had better say 'that I *should*, *if* I had chosen'. In other words, the suggestion is that we often use the phrase 'I *could*' simply and solely as a short way of saying 'I *should*, if I had chosen'.[7]

Agreeing with Roderick Chisholm,[8] and relying on what I will call Moore's official account of his intention in the above passage, I believe that Moore was concerned in *Ethics* with analyzing—not completing or expanding—a sentence such as "Moore could have walked a mile in twenty minutes this morning". After all, Moore suggests in this passage—after speaking parenthetically of avoiding a possible complication—that perhaps we had better say that "I could do so-and-so" is a short way of saying "I should have done so-and-so if I had chosen"; and this synonymy underlies an analysis rather than a completion of "I could do so-and-so" since what Moore regards as the long way here does not contain the word "could", as it should in the case of an expansion and as it should not in the case of an analysis. That is why I think that the third-person analysan-

[7] Ibid., p. 131.
[8] Review of Austin's *Philosophical Papers*, *Mind* 73 (1964): 21–22.

dum, "Moore could have walked a mile in twenty minutes this morning", is held by Moore to be a complete statement that is analyzed by what Moore must have regarded as the logically more complex, complete, third-person analysans, "If Moore had chosen to walk a mile in twenty minutes this morning, Moore would have walked a mile in twenty minutes this morning". Moore holds something analogous about the statement "Moore can walk a mile in twenty minutes this morning".

However, if Moore holds that "Moore can walk a mile in twenty minutes this morning" is a complete sentence, what should he say about the conditional statement "Moore *can* walk a mile in twenty minutes this morning if he chooses"? Not, obviously, that it is the completion of "Moore can walk a mile in twenty minutes this morning" if the latter is supposed by him to be complete. It would have been better for Moore to have said, as Donald Davidson does,[9] that this conditional statement is logically equivalent to "Moore can walk a mile in twenty minutes this morning" and not that it presents its analysis, since Moore holds that the latter is to be analyzed as meaning the same as "Moore *will* walk a mile in twenty minutes this morning if he chooses", and since he usually distinguishes between saying that two sentences are logically equivalent and saying that one presents the analysis of the other.

To see this logical equivalence, we must first observe, in accordance with what Davidson says,[10] that the following logical equivalence is a law of the sentential calculus:

(1) (If p, then q) if and only if (If p, then if p, then q).

Now let us abbreviate our sentences, using "Moore walks" as short for "Moore walks (will walk) a mile in twenty min-

[9] Davidson, "Freedom to Act," p. 66.
[10] Ibid., pp. 66–67.

utes this morning" and "Moore chooses" as short for "Moore chooses to walk a mile in twenty minutes this morning". Using these abbreviations, we can substitute in (1) to get:

(2) (If Moore chooses, then Moore walks) if and only if (If Moore chooses, then if Moore chooses, then Moore walks).

Next we use Moore's suggested analysis of "Moore can walk" in *Ethics*:

(3) "Moore can walk" is synonymous with "If Moore chooses, then Moore walks".

Putting (3)'s left-hand analysandum for its right-hand analysans in (2), we derive the following logical equivalence from (2):

(4) (If Moore chooses, then Moore walks) if and only if (If Moore chooses, then Moore can walk).

According to this argument, "Moore can walk", "Moore can walk if he chooses", and "Moore walks (will walk) if he chooses" are logically equivalent. But this is not to say that we can *analyze* "Moore can walk", as Moore understands "analyze", by presenting the sentence "Moore can walk if he chooses". That they are logically equivalent does not mean that the second gives an analysis of the former, as we can see from the fact that "Ivan Karamazov is a brother" is logically equivalent to "Ivan Karamazov is a brother and Ivan Karamazov is a brother" without the latter presenting an analysis of the former. By contrast, "Ivan Karamazov is a brother" is analyzed by "Ivan Karamazov is a male sibling" or by "Ivan Karamazov is a male and Ivan Karamazov is a sibling". In this case the analysans is a sentence that contains "male", "sibling", and the "and" of logical conjunction, but not "brother". Yet this is not true of "Ivan Karamazov is a brother and Ivan Karamazov is a brother", which is not an analysis of "brother" if only because it does not contain any predicate other than "brother".[11]

All of this supports the claim that Moore best states his view of the sentence "Moore can walk" when he says that it is to be analyzed as meaning the same as "Moore walks (or will walk) if he chooses". Showing, as Davidson does, that "Moore can walk" is therefore logically equivalent to "Moore can walk if he chooses" permits Davidson to refute some things that Austin says about Moore's view and to defend Moore's right to put "Moore can walk if he chooses" for "Moore can walk" in contexts where logical equivalence suffices. I repeat, however, that this does not show that "Moore can walk" may be analyzed in Moore's sense by saying "Moore can walk if he chooses".

I should add that Moore is not alone in his tendency to say that "I can" is synonymous with "I can if I choose" or similar sentences, nor in his tendency to use the first person in place of the third when illustrating what it is to have free will or liberty. Both tendencies are present, for example, in Hobbes, who says: "I acknowledge this *liberty*, that I *can* do if I *will*".[12] The first tendency is present in Locke, who says: "a Man that sits still, is said yet to be at liberty, because he can walk if he *wills* it";[13] and in Hume, who says something similar while replacing "can" by "may":

[11] Having said this, I should point out that Moore denies that giving an analysis is saying that a linguistic expression such as "Ivan Karamazov is a brother" has the same meaning as "Ivan Karamazov is a male sibling". Instead, Moore insisted, we analyze the concept or attribute of being a brother as being identical with that of being a male sibling. See *The Philosophy of G. E. Moore*, ed. P. A. Schilpp, esp. pp. 661–62.

[12] Hobbes, "Of Liberty and Necessity", *Works*, ed. W. Molesworth (London: Bohn, 1840; repr. 1966), Vol. 4, p. 240.

[13] Locke, *An Essay Concerning Human Understanding*, p. 246.

"By liberty, . . . we can only mean *a power of acting or not acting, according to the determinations of the will*; that is, if we choose to remain at rest, we may; if we choose to move, we also may".[14]

3. Does "He Is Free to A" Logically Imply "He Can Choose to A"?

Now I wish to turn to a much more serious problem that emerges in the literature on Moore's effort to analyze sentences such as "Cicero can kill Caesar", one which leads me to add some further reflections on the merit of adding "Cicero can choose to kill Caesar" to "If Cicero chooses to kill Caesar, he will kill him" in the analysis of "Cicero can kill Caesar". Davidson praises Chisholm for holding "that while it might be true that if a man were to choose, or try, to perform some action, then he would perform that action, nevertheless he might be unable to choose or to try, in which case he couldn't perform the action. So it might be true that a person would _____ if he tried, yet false that he could _____. . . . What the argument shows is that the antecedent of a causal conditional that attempts to analyze 'can' or 'could' or 'free to' must not contain, as its dominant verb, a verb of action, or any verb which makes sense of the question, Can someone do *it*?".[15] On the basis of what I have said earlier, the reader will know that I agree with everything in the quotation that precedes the words "what the argument shows". For this is a generalization of Garnett's point that it would be false to say that a person

---

[14] Hume, *Enquiry concerning Human Understanding*, in *Hume's Enquiries*, ed. L. A. Selby-Bigge, p. 95.
[15] Davidson, "Freedom to Act", p. 68.

could have avoided performing an action if that person could not have chosen to avoid performing it. But I disagree with the rest of the quotation because it forbids our saying that "Cicero can kill Caesar" may be analyzed as meaning the same as the conjunction "If Cicero chooses to kill Caesar, he will kill him; and Cicero can choose to kill Caesar". Consequently, it forbids our analyzing "Cicero is free to kill Caesar" as synonymous with "Cicero can kill Caesar and Cicero can not kill Caesar" (where we must put a space between "can" and "not" for obvious reasons);[16] and it forbids our analyzing this two-part conjunction as synonymous with the four-part conjunction "If Cicero chooses to kill Caesar, he will kill him; and he can choose to kill Caesar; and if he chooses not to kill Caesar, he will not kill him; and he can choose not to kill Caesar".

Instead of saying that the antecedent of a causal conditional statement that attempts to analyze "can" or "could" or "free to" must not contain as its dominant verb a verb of action, or any verb which makes sense of the question "Can someone do it?", I allow the antecedent of a causal conditional statement to contain such a verb while regarding this causal conditional as only one conjunct of the analysis of "Cicero can kill Caesar".

It is now important to say something further about the view that the effort to analyze "can" in terms of "will if" is bound to fail because, to repeat Davidson's words, "while it might be true that if a man were to choose, or try, to perform some action, then he would perform that action, nevertheless he might be unable to choose or to try, in which case, he couldn't perform the action". According to

---

[16] The point is that "Brutus cannot kill Caesar" is quite different from "Brutus can avoid killing Caesar", which is synonymous with "Brutus can not kill Caesar", where "can" and "not" have a space between them.

Chisholm, this "confirms Austin's profound remark: 'In philosophy it is *can* in particular that we seem so often to uncover, just when we had thought some problem settled, grinning residually up at us like the frog at the bottom of the beer mug'".[17] With this in mind I want to emphasize that because the view I favor permits us to analyze "He can perform *A*" as a conjunction of "If he chooses to perform *A*, he will perform *A*" and "He can choose to perform *A*", it eliminates Austin's frog by eliminating "He can choose to perform *A*" in favor of a statement that does not contain "can", that is, by a sentence which says that the agent's not choosing to perform *A* is not necessitated by a certain event or by a certain kind of event.

If this view is correct, we need not deny, as Davidson does, that a verb such as "choose" may be used in the antecedent of a causal conditional that is a conjunct in the analysans of "Cicero can kill Caesar". Davidson writes: "The only hope for the causal analysis is to find states or events ... which are not themselves actions or events about which the question whether the agent can perform them can intelligibly be raised".[18] I think he says this because he thinks that the fact that we may intelligibly ask the question "Can Cicero choose to kill Caesar?" and that we must answer it affirmatively if we wish to say that Cicero can kill Caesar, shows that we do not eliminate "can" when we analyze "Cicero can kill Caesar" as meaning the same as "If Cicero chooses to kill Caesar, he will kill him". But if, by expansion and analysis, we transform "Cicero can kill Caesar" into, for example, the conjunction "If Cicero chooses to kill Caesar, he will kill him; and Cicero's

---

[17] See Chisholm, review of Austin, p. 25; Austin, *Philosophical Papers*, p. 179.

[18] Davidson, "Freedom to Act", p. 72.

not choosing to kill Caesar is not causally necessitated by the operation on Cicero of an absolute precluder of choice", the second conjunct will be our answer to the question: "What is meant by 'Cicero can choose to kill Caesar'?" and our way of eliminating the frog.

4. REMARKS ON POSSIBLE OPPORTUNITIES

Although I have argued that we must add that Cicero can choose to kill Caesar if we wish to analyze "Cicero can kill Caesar" by presenting "If Cicero chooses to kill Caesar, then Cicero kills Caesar" as part of the analysis, we should bear in mind that a sentence such as "Cicero can kill Caesar" or "Moore could have walked a mile in twenty minutes this morning" may be analyzed in certain circumstances with the help of a conditional statement which has a different sort of antecedent. For example, the statement about Moore's possible walk might, in certain circumstances, be analyzed as meaning the same as:

(1) If Moore had not had a blister on his right foot this morning, he would have walked a mile in twenty minutes this morning; and it was possible for Moore not to have had a blister on his right foot this morning.

If we deny the second conjunct, we must, in accordance with what we have seen in the previous section, deny that Moore could have walked a mile in twenty minutes this morning, whether the antecedent of the conditional statement refers to a choice made by the agent or to a state in which he is. Therefore, the general statement to be made about such an antecedent is not "The agent can do that" since this will not be in order when the antecedent refers to a state in which the agent is, a state such as Moore's not having had a blister on his right foot.

Let us pursue the matter a bit further by supposing that Moore's failure to walk a mile in twenty minutes this morning had been morally condemned as a violation of Moore's obligation to walk a twenty-minute mile this morning because of a promise on his part to do so. We may imagine someone saying that Moore was not morally obligated to walk a twenty-minute mile this morning because it was impossible for him not to have had a blister on his right foot this morning and therefore impossible for him to have walked a mile in twenty minutes this morning. This shows that we may deny that Moore had an obligation to do something on the ground that Moore could not be in a certain state, just as we may deny it on the ground that Moore could not make a certain choice. Consequently, it shows that in certain circumstances we may replace "Moore could have walked a mile in twenty minutes this morning" by statement (1) above. I also think it shows that "Moore could have walked a mile in twenty minutes this morning" may in certain circumstances be replaced by:

(2) If Moore had had the opportunity to walk a mile in twenty minutes this morning, he would have walked a mile in twenty minutes this morning; and Moore could have had the opportunity to walk a mile in twenty minutes this morning.

Therefore, the possibility-conjunct we add to a conditional statement in the analysans of "Moore could have walked a mile in twenty minutes this morning" may assert possibility either by asserting the possibility of Moore's having made a choice or the possibility of Moore's having had an opportunity or being in a certain state. I do not wish at this point to launch an inquiry into the difficult notion of opportunity or into the more difficult notion that might be called "freedom of opportunity", but I do wish to make a very important digression and an equally important admission.

5. A Digression

What I have just been saying may be compared with the view that some conditional statements that appear in the analysis of singular "could have"-statements may have the form of "If that match had been struck, it would have lit" whereas others may have the form of "If that match had been dry, it would have lit". The first conditional statement might be asserted by a person who believes that an unstruck match was dry and surrounded by the requisite amount of oxygen; the second by a person who believes that a struck match was surrounded by the requisite amount of oxygen but wet. Either one of these conditional statements might appear—on different occasions—in an analysis of "That match could have lit", where the conditional statement was conjoined in each case with a statement of possibility. In the first case we would add "That match could have been struck"; in the second case we would add "That match could have been dry".

However, when we are talking about the lighting of a match as opposed to the action of a person, the statement "That match could have been dry" must be distinguished in one important respect from "Moore could have had the opportunity to walk a mile in twenty minutes this morning". The point is that the denial of "Moore could have had the opportunity to walk a mile in twenty minutes this

morning" morally implies the denial of the moral statement "Moore ought to have walked a mile in twenty minutes this morning"—meaning that the conditional whose
antecedent is the first denial and whose consequent is the
second is a moral truth—whereas, of course, the denial of
the statement "That match could have been dry" does not
morally imply the denial of "That match had a moral obligation to light". For this reason, the question about appropriate precluders that arises when we try to interpret
"Moore could have had the opportunity to walk a mile in
twenty minutes this morning" has no counterpart in the
case of "That match could have been dry". It is obviously
very important to realize, therefore, that we cannot use the
moral dictum that "Ought" implies "Can" in trying to say
which precluder or precluders of the match's dryness prevent its being dry.[19]

All of this seems to show that we should refrain from
using some of the main ideas of this study when trying to
deal with statements such as "This match can light" or
"That match could have lit". Let me explain the sort of
thing I have in mind. A match could be lying on the floor
of a Berkeleian forest in which no human being is present
to strike the match. Nevertheless, we might say "That
match could have lit"; and we might also say that the latter
sentence is to be analyzed as meaning the same as "If that
match had been struck by lightning, it would have lit". If
we did say this, a philosopher might correctly point out
that even if this conditional statement were true, it would
be false to say that the match could have lit if it were im-

---

[19] "When we have the course of nature alone in view, '*ought*' has no
meaning whatsoever. It is just as absurd to ask what ought to happen in
the natural world as to ask what properties a circle ought to have", Kant,
Critique of Pure Reason, ed. N. Kemp-Smith (London: Macmillan, 1950),
p. 473; A547–B575. I came upon this while examining some passages in
Kant to which Robert Howell had kindly referred me.

possible for the match to have been struck by lightning. In that case we may ask: Would it be in order to bring to bear the sort of expansion and analysis I have used earlier? Would it be in order to include in our analysis of "That match could have lit" the statement "It is possible that the match could have been struck by lightning", and then to expand and analyze that statement as I have suggested that we expand and analyze "Cicero could have chosen to kill Caesar"? I think not, simply because we would not be able to use the dictum that "Ought" morally implies "Can" and its corollary that "Cannot" morally implies "Not ought", and therefore we would not be able to test supposedly appropriate precluders as we do in the case of "Cicero could have chosen to kill Caesar". As we saw earlier, it would make no sense to affirm or deny "That match had a moral obligation to light". We would not be able to use my method of saying which of the many possible precluders of the match's being struck by lightning are appropriate, because it would make no sense to say that any of them would relieve the match of an obligation to light.

Under the circumstances I want to acknowledge that my efforts in this study are not aimed at solving the problem of analyzing statements like "That match could have lit" as opposed to those like "Cicero could have killed Caesar". I do not know how to test supposedly appropriate precluders of a match's being struck by lightning because I do not know of anything like the principle that every obligatory action is free to which I can turn. If I try to analyze "That match could have lit" by first offering the conditional statement "If that match had been struck by lightning, it would have lit" and am then brought up short by someone who says that the match could not have lit because it could not have been struck by lightning, I have no views ready on how to expand and analyze "It could have been struck by lightning". Nevertheless, I do not think that this militates against the views I have advanced on how to expand and analyze "Cicero could have killed Caesar". Nor do I think that it militates against the view that the statement "That match could have been struck by lightning" means the same as a statement which says that such-and-such did not causally necessitate the match's not being struck by lightning. The problem is to say what should replace "such-and-such". Maybe the only thing to say here is that whoever says that that match could have been struck by lightning should tell us what precluder or sort of precluder he has in mind.

6. Further Remarks on Possible Opportunities

Let me now return to my reflections upon what may be called "freedom of opportunity" in cases where it does make sense to speak of moral obligations. I admit, of course, that a sentence such as "Cicero could have killed Caesar" is not usually analyzed by theorists of free will as being synonymous with "If Cicero had had the opportunity to kill Caesar, he would have killed him". Instead, as we know, they analyze it with the help of a sentence like "If Cicero had chosen to kill Caesar, he would have killed him," which gives rise to the question: "But *could* Cicero have chosen to kill Caesar?" and thence to the sort of debate that I have considered at sufficient length. In my opinion, however, a similar debate can be generated by focusing on a causal conditional statement such as "If Cicero had had the opportunity to kill Caesar, he would have killed him". Here, as we have seen, the next question to ask is: "But *could* Cicero have had the opportunity to kill Caesar?" or "Was it possible for Cicero to have had the opportunity?", which I think can inaugurate a similar discussion. If someone were to argue that Cicero could have had the opportunity, he would properly be asked what he means by "could" and properly be told that if it were impossible for Cicero to have had the opportunity to kill Caesar, then Cicero could not have killed him even if were true that if Cicero had had the opportunity to kill Caesar, he would have killed Caesar. Here too, however, it would be in order to say that the statement "Cicero could have killed Caesar" is not synonymous with "If Cicero had had the opportunity to kill Caesar, he would have killed him" alone but that it is synonymous with the conjunction of that conditional statement and "It was possible for Cicero to have had the opportunity to kill Caesar", when the last sentence elliptically says that Cicero's not having that opportunity had not been necessitated.

Since I have not been concerned in this study with this sort of elliptical denial of necessitation, I have not said anything about what appropriate precluders of opportunity we should exclude when analyzing the statement that Cicero could have had the opportunity. Indeed, I am not sure what opportunity-precluders would correspond to such things as an attack of epileptic automatism, to being drugged, and to being hypnotized when we are discussing appropriate preclusion of choice. But I suspect that there are philosophical issues here which are analogous to those that arise in the case of choice, and therefore that the situation here is different from what it is in the case of the match in the Berkeleian forest. It would seem that philosophers have not faced these issues because they have been less interested in debating whether Cicero could have had the opportunity to kill Caesar than in debating whether Cicero could have chosen to kill Caesar. The latter debate concerns what could be willed, and so, naturally, philosophers interested in free *will* have been more given to debating whether choosing is determined than in debating whether having an opportunity is determined. Moreover, philosophers have not been given to saying that there are uncaused or undetermined opportunities, and for this reason, perhaps, the notion of a possible opportunity has not attracted a school of antideterminists who say something analogous to what antideterminists say about choice.

It should be noted—in light of earlier remarks in this chapter—that when the philosopher neglects to add that it was possible for Cicero to have made the choice, we can recommend adding the intelligible sentence "Cicero could have performed the act of making the choice", but that when he neglects to add that it was possible for Cicero to have had the opportunity, we cannot intelligibly recommend adding "Cicero could have performed the act of having the opportunity". Yet we can intelligibly recommend adding "It was possible for Cicero to have had the opportunity to kill Caesar", and then expand and analyze this elliptical sentence in a way that allows us to assert that its denial will morally imply the denial of "Cicero had a duty to kill Caesar". However, I should repeat that although we may rely here on a moral judgment in determining what expansion and analysis of the statement "Cicero could not have had the opportunity to kill Caesar" is a basis for denying "Cicero had a duty to kill him", the first statement is nonetheless factual, just as "Cicero could not have chosen to kill Caesar" is. I stress this last point because, as I have said earlier, I do not wish to be understood to hold that the moral implication of "free" by "ought" makes "Cicero was free to kill Caesar" a moral statement. It is as descriptive as any statement that refers to an act that is morally required or prohibited, for example, "Hea honored his parents",

"Hea stole the watch", and "Hea killed Shea". For this reason the moral conditional statement "If Cicero ought to kill Caesar, then Cicero can kill Caesar" is not one whose antecedent and consequent are both moral. The same is true, of course, of the moral conditional statement "If Brutus killed Caesar, then Brutus did something he ought to have done".

Holism, Corporatism, and the Problem of Free Will

IN THIS CHAPTER I want to compare certain expansions and analyses of "Cicero can kill Caesar" and "Cicero can choose to kill Caesar"; and since the results of these transformations will appear in conjunctions of statements, my comparisons will deal with conjunctions. In making these comparisons, I will apply holistic or corporatist epistemology to different theories of free will as I think it should be applied when we compare two rival theories in science. Just as the heliocentric theory consists of a conjunction of statements that is scientifically preferable to the geocentric theory, and just as Darwin's theory of evolution through natural selection consists of a conjunction that is scientifically superior to one that embodies Lamarck's theory of evolution, so I believe that one sort of theory or conjunction about free will is preferable to another. And because the moral statement that we have a duty to do only what we are free to do is a central component in such conjunctions, they will be heterogeneous by virtue of containing both moral and nonmoral, that is to say descriptive, components. Therefore, any comparison of such rival heterogeneous conjunctions should be made by consulting our sensory experiences *and* our moral feelings, which are emotional experiences, and not by consulting our sensory experiences alone. It should also be made by comparing the extent to which such theories preserve beliefs that we are reluctant to reject or revise, as well as the simplicity of such theories.

1. HOLISM AND CORPORATISM

We may better understand the testing of rival conjunctions that contain both descriptive and moral statements by first examining the testing of conjunctions that are exclusively descriptive and therefore tested in what Quine calls a holistic manner. The basic idea of Quine's holism and that of his forerunner Duhem is that we test statements in bunches rather than in isolation. Holism says that such a bunch, body, or conjunction should face sensory experience collectively when we test a theory, and that when the conjunction is confronted by a sensory experience that goes against it, the resulting difficulty may be dealt with in different ways. Once we recognize that we are testing a conjunction of statements which implies reports of sensory experience, we can see that any sensory experience which leads us to deny the conjunction will lead us to deny at least one of the conjuncts. If we believe that all crows are pink and that Courtney is a crow, then a certain principle of logic will lead us to conclude that Courtney is pink. But if we look at Courtney in white light, and our eyes are normal, and Courtney seems to us not to be pink, we may try to accommodate our adverse experience in different ways. We may reject our belief that all crows are pink; we may reject our belief that Courtney is a crow; or we may reject the logical beliefs that governed our original deduction; or, of course, we may reject all of these beliefs. Quine once said that the body of beliefs which is subject to rejection or alteration is the entire body of science, but more recently he has said what Duhem was inclined to say: that the tested conjunction consists of "more modest chunks" of belief that are used together in order to predict what is experienced.[1]

Whether a holist applies his epistemology to the totality of scientific beliefs or to a smaller group, that group may consist of different kinds of beliefs; for example, some may come from biology, some from mathematics, and some from logic. This may be illustrated with the help of my simple example if one regards the statement that all crows are pink and the statement that Courtney is a crow as biological statements, and if one regards the principle that leads from the conjunction of them to the statement that Courtney is pink as a logical statement. In reflecting on this illustration, holists may differ about whether a logical statement or belief may be rejected on the basis of sensory experience. Some may insist that only beliefs in natural science—for example, in biology or physics—may be rejected in response to such an experience whereas mathematical and logical beliefs may not be rejected in this way; others may hold that any component of a body of beliefs may be removed from that body in response to an adverse experience. Thus Duhem believed that sensory experience may be used to reject beliefs in natural science and not the truths of pure mathematics or logic, whereas Quine has held that not only beliefs in natural science but also beliefs in logic, mathematics, and ontology may be put in jeopardy when we engage in testing by observation or experiment. Since I include moral beliefs among testable conjunctions of beliefs, I further expand the limits of the class

---

[1] Quine's earlier version of his holism is presented in his paper, "Two Dogmas of Empiricism"; he presents his later view in "Five Milestones of Empiricism".

of beliefs that may be tested by experience. I adopt what I have called methodological monism when I treat normative ethics and label my view "corporatism" in order to distinguish it from other varieties of holism because I also include certain emotional experiences or moral feelings among those that may lead us to reject or revise our theories.[2]

Suppose, for example, that someone says that all acts of a certain kind ought to be performed, that a particular act is of that kind, and therefore that the act ought to be performed. If we reject the conclusion of this argument because it is not in accord with our emotional experience, we may reject either one of the premises or the logical principle employed in the reasoning from the premises to the conclusion. The singular conclusion that the act ought to be performed may be rejected as a consequence of a recalcitrant emotional experience that stands to it as a recalcitrant sensory experience may stand to "Courtney is pink". In testing the body of beliefs that includes "Courtney is pink", we may add to that body the statement "Whenever a pink object is observed by a normal person in white light, it seems pink to that person", so if Courtney does not appear pink to us, we may reject any one of the premises that lead to the conclusion that he does appear pink to us.

When discussing this topic in an earlier work, I did not say that the moral conclusion that an act ought to be performed might be rejected on the basis of experience but said rather that it might be rejected on the basis of experience and emotion or feeling.[3] I now think it preferable to say that a person may reject this conclusion on the basis of sensory and emotional experience. The purpose of this

---

[2] My views are presented in *What Is and What Ought To Be Done*, esp. chapter 2.

[3] Ibid., esp. chapter 3.

change in terminology is to emphasize that a feeling or an emotion is also an experience. According to this terminology, the general statement: "Every act that ought to be performed is one which a normal person will feel obligated to perform when that person considers the act while in a normal state" is just as experiential as the statement: "Whenever a pink object is observed by a normal person in white light, it looks pink to that person". In the first case we describe how certain acts will strike certain kinds of persons when they are in certain circumstances; in the second we describe how physical objects will strike certain kinds of persons when *they* are in certain circumstances. Consequently, the conjunction of the first general statement above with the statement that a particular act ought to be performed logically implies that a normal person will experience a feeling of moral obligation; and the conjunction of the second general statement and "Courtney is pink" logically implies that a normal person will have a certain sensory experience. I realize that some philosophers might not agree that there are feelings of obligation, but I think that such feelings exist and that they play a part in moral thinking that is analogous to the part played by sensory experiences in the thinking of the purely descriptive scientist; a moral feeling, like a sensory experience, may conflict with the conclusion of a hypothetico-deductive argument and lead a thinker to reject or revise at least one of his premises. I might add parenthetically that a holist who is an ethical naturalist, or one who believes that ethics may be reduced to a natural science because he thinks that "ought"-statements are analyzable into statements of the natural science of psychology, might say that an argument from a moral principle and a singular statement of fact to a singular moral conclusion should be tested holistically by appealing to sensory experience alone. Such a philosopher, if he is a utilitarian and a naturalist, will test a typical ethical argument from a moral principle and a singular descriptive statement to a singular moral conclusion just as he tests the argument from "All crows are pink and Courtney is a crow" to "Courtney is pink" since his utilitarianism will lead to his translating the moral principle into a statement of psychology. So, if the result of this test is negative, then the ethical naturalist who is a holist will reject or revise his set of premises just as our biologist did earlier.

When Duhem asked how we decide which beliefs in a conjunction we should reject or revise if the conjunction implies a report that comes in conflict with experience, he said that we should not expect to find an absolute principle that will help us decide. Instead, he spoke of Pascalian "reasons which reason does not know" as constituting "what is appropriately called good sense" about these matters.[4] But when William James dealt with a similar question, he spoke more circumstantially of the need to deal with a conflict with experience by minimally disturbing what he called "the ancient stock" of opinions and by keeping in mind the need to keep one's theory simple, economical, or elegant.[5] In my view, we should proceed similarly when we evaluate the partly moral, partly descriptive conjunctions that philosophers assert when dealing with free will. We should require that these conjunctions be in accord with experience; that, as James said, they "derange common sense and previous belief as little as possible"; and that they be simple, economical, or elegant. And just as a purely descriptive theory is in my view dedicated to organizing a stream of sensory experience

---

[4] Duhem, *The Aim and Structure of Physical Theory*, p. 217.

[5] William James, *Pragmatism* (Cambridge, Mass.: Harvard University Press, 1975), p. 104.

alone, so a partly moral, partly descriptive theory should organize a stream of sensory and emotional or moral experiences. I realize that this leaves many other questions to be answered concerning the method of such organization but since I have dealt with such questions elsewhere, I will not dilate on them here.[6] To do so would take me too far from my immediate concern, which is to show how the claims of experience, conservatism, and simplicity may be appealed to when we are comparing rival theories about free will.

2. Two Rival Conjunctions

Now I want to apply these requirements to the problems concerning free will by making comparisons that I mentioned earlier. To make the first of these comparisons in some detail, I will recapitulate two opposing theories that I have discussed earlier, omitting, however, the logical principles that might have been included by a thoroughgoing holist as components of these theories. I want to compare in a holistic manner two theories that differ insofar as one of them says that possible choices are those that are not precluded by anything whereas the other says that possible choices are those that are not precluded by such things as drugging, disease, or hypnosis.

I start by formulating a theory that begins with a moral argument that leads to the moral conclusion (sentence (v) below) that Cicero ought to kill Caesar, a conclusion that I assume was made before Caesar was killed by others. I also assume that Cicero did not choose to kill Caesar and did not kill Caesar, and state this in sentence (o). From the

[6] See n. 2 above.

moral conclusion that Cicero ought to kill Caesar the theory derives the further conclusion that Cicero is free to kill Caesar (sentence (vii)), which leads by way of an analysis of freedom (viii) to the statement that Cicero can choose to kill Caesar (sentence (ix)). After this sentence, which is a crucial point in the argument, the rival theories diverge. It should be noted, however, that before the divergence both of the rival theorists infer "Cicero is free to kill Caesar" from "Cicero ought to kill Caesar", though I emphasize that philosophers who make this inference may do so on different grounds. I also wish to point out that some philosophers may not make this inference, in which case they may begin the argument below with the assertion "Cicero is free to kill Caesar". They may wish to avoid the whole business of deriving this statement from a moral statement because they think it obvious that some actions are free, but I find it hard to see why a philosopher should make this statement without thinking of it as connected in some way with morality, especially a philosopher who is not a theist and who is not motivated by a desire to know how man's freedom is related to God's presumed omnipotence.[7]

I present now the theory that begins as an argument for a moral conclusion and then reaches a fork where two roads go in different directions. Reasons for steps are given in brackets:

(o) Cicero did not choose to kill Caesar and did not kill him. [Descriptive statement of fact]

---

[7] I do not have in mind here the sort of freedom discussed in Mill's essay *On Liberty*. Mill says at the very beginning of that essay that "the subject of this essay is not the so-called liberty of the will . . . ; but the civil or social liberty: the nature and limits of the power which can be legitimately exercised by society over the individual".

(i) Every citizen who has the opportunity to kill a' ty-rant ought to kill him. [Moral principle]
(ii) Caesar is a tyrant. [Descriptive statement of fact]
(iii) Cicero is a citizen. [Descriptive statement of fact]
(iv) Cicero has an opportunity to kill Caesar. [De-scriptive statement of fact]

Therefore,

(v) Cicero ought to kill Caesar. [(i), (ii), (iii), (iv), and a principle of logic]

At this point in the argument, the philosopher takes a step for which he may give different reasons. As we have seen earlier, he may make statement (vi) below on the ground that it is a so-called rational principle, a so-called "conceptual truth", or a statement whose denial is non-sensical. Or he may hold, as I do, that it is a contingent moral principle that may be denied without contradicting oneself or lapsing into nonsense. Therefore, as I have said, the important philosophical difference about the step im-mediately after (v) is not about what statement to make but rather about what reason to give for it, which is why I offer two alternative reasons in the next set of brackets:

(vi) Whoever ought to kill a person is free to kill that person. [Moral principle or rational principle]

Therefore,

(vii) Cicero is free to kill Caesar. [(v), (vi), and a princi-ple of logic]

The next step reflects an analysis of free action:

(viii) If Cicero chooses to kill Caesar, he will kill him; and Cicero can choose to kill Caesar; and if Cicero chooses not to kill Caesar, he will not kill him; and

Cicero can choose not to kill Caesar. [(vii) and the analysis of "free" that I favor]

Therefore,

(ix) Cicero can choose to kill Caesar [(viii) and a principle of logic].

The argument as presented thus far may be accepted by two opposing theorists of free will. Although, in their next steps, these opposing theorists will reveal their colors more conspicuously, the philosopher who analyzes a possible choice as one that is not precluded by specific factors may reveal his conception of possible choice in at least two ways. He may, for example, make statement (x) after (ix) if he thinks (ix) should be expanded into a denial of a specific assertion of causal necessitation and if he also thinks he has a general criterion—for example, that of absolute preclusion—for picking out what I have earlier called appropriate precluders of choice:

(x) Cicero's not choosing to kill Caesar is not causally necessitated by an event which is an absolute precluder of Cicero's choice. [By expansion and analysis of (ix)]

Alternatively, this sort of philosopher may infer statement (x*) from (ix) because he thinks that (ix) should be expanded into a denial of specific necessitation. But this philosopher *lists* the sorts of events that do not causally necessitate Cicero's not choosing to kill Caesar instead of offering a general characterization of those events:

(x*) Cicero's not choosing to kill Caesar is not causally necessitated by Cicero's having undergone an attack of epileptic automatism, by his having been hypnotized by another without his cooperation, or by his having been appropriately drugged by another without his cooperation. [By expansion and analysis of (ix)]

It is worth adding that this same philosopher may derive from (ix) a statement that differs from (x) insofar as he replaces the expression "an absolute precluder" in (x) by some other general term such as "external precluder"; or he may make a statement that differs from (x*) in listing nonnecessitators of Cicero's not choosing to kill Caesar that differ from those listed in (x*). It is also worth adding that although this philosopher may be a determinist, he need not be so far as his argument here is concerned, for at no point in it does he assert or logically imply the truth of universal causation or determinism. However, he does interpret "Cicero can choose to kill Caesar" in a way that avoids making his rival's antideterministic assertion of (x') below.

It is obvious why statements like (x) and (x*) suit the philosopher who does not wish to abandon or to assert determinism while interpreting a sentence such as "Cicero can choose to kill Caesar". Each of these statements represents a way of completing an elliptical denial of causal necessitation so that it does not logically imply the falsehood of the principle of universal causal necessitation. But a difficult question will remain for the philosopher even after deciding that he should follow the pattern of (x) or (x*). He will have to select a particular example of this pattern, and in doing so will continue to be guided by his understanding of "free" in statement (vi): "Whoever ought to kill a person is free to kill that person". The philosopher who does not reject determinism will need to make this selection because he may disagree with another who is equally averse to rejecting determinism but who offers a different interpretation of the word "free" in statement (vi). For example, one philosopher who accepts the pattern of (x*) may regard only an attack of a particular choice-preventing disease as an appropriate precluder whereas another who accepts the pattern of (x*) may wish to add to this precluder one or both of the other precluders—hypnosis and drugging—that are listed in (x*) as it now stands.

The antideterminist who supports his view by taking steps (o) through (ix) will of course be guided by his understanding of statement (vi), but he will infer that for Cicero's choice to be possible as stated in (ix), its not being made must not be caused by *anything*. Many philosophers hold that a correct interpretation of (vi) requires this, and therefore, after moving from (o) through (ix) in the above argument, they will decline to take the step to (x) or (x*) and will insist that the appropriate step from (ix) is:

(x′) Cicero's not choosing to kill Caesar is not causally necessitated by some (any) other event. [By expansion and analysis of (ix)].

And from (x′) antideterminists deduce a corollary of their denial of determinism or of universal causal necessitation:

(xi) Not every event in the history of a person is causally necessitated by some other event. [(x′) and logic]

This antideterminist presumably understands the principle of universal causation to say that for every event in the history of a thing, whether that thing be a match or a person, there is an event that causally necessitates the first event. According to this principle, if we say that a match lit because it was struck and are asked whether something caused the striking, then, if we answer in the affirmative without knowing what caused the striking, we may do so because we accept universal causation or determinism. The antideterminist represented above rejects this principle because he says that Cicero's not choosing to kill Caesar is not causally necessitated by anything.

3. Comparing These Two Rivals

We now see that the different theories to be compared are as follows: one of them is the conjunction asserted by the antideterminist who asserts (x′), and the other is a conjunction that differs from the first by virtue of containing a statement such as (x) or (x*) in place of (x′). Once the opponent of antideterminism—who, as I have said, need not accept determinism—fixes on the conjunction he wishes to assert by deciding whether he wishes to assert something like (x) or something like (x*), we have before us two theories that may be compared for their capacity to organize our sensory and emotional experiences, for their capacity to avoid excessive tampering with what James calls the "older truths", and for their degree of simplicity or elegance. Consequently, the fundamental question is this: Which of the compared theories or conjunctions better meets these three requirements?

I think that the theory which logically implies a statement like (x) or (x*) is in accord with experience whereas the theory that logically implies (x′) and antideterminism stands in a problematic relationship to experience. If we accept (x) and assert that no event which is an absolute precluder of choice causally necessitates Cicero's not choosing to kill Caesar, then we will be able to say truly that one person can choose to kill another whereas another cannot, and that one person can so choose at one time but not at another. Because some choices are not absolutely precluded and some are, the acceptance of (x) as an interpretation of (ix) will be in accord with the commonly accepted fact that some persons can choose to kill Caesar whereas others cannot, and with the fact that a given person can choose to kill Caesar at one time but not be able to make this choice at another. The same may be said of (x*) as an interpretation of (ix), so that theories of free will containing either (x) or (x*) will be in accord with our experience in this respect. They will be in accord with our common sense empirical belief that some choices are possible and others not.

By contrast, the situation is quite different when we accept (x′) as an interpretation of "Cicero can choose to kill Caesar". No matter what person and what choice we speak about in an argument that is analogous to the one running from (o) through (x′), the counterpart of (x′) will always be true. In other words, whoever the person may be and whatever his choice may be, it will be true to say that he can make that choice. And this, I repeat, is contrary to our experience when we speak of choices made by human beings and use the word "choice" as we normally do. I conclude therefore that when we apply the most important of James's canons—the one that requires us to organize our experiences—the theory of the philosopher who does not reject determinism comes off better than the theory of the antideterminist.

Next let us apply James's principle of conservatism, the one that urges respect for James's "ancient stock" of opinions. When I apply it during this comparison, I conclude that the theory which contains (x) or (x*) should be given points for not taking a stand on the principle of determinism, but I want to emphasize an important asymmetry in the rival theories. Whereas the philosopher who accepts (x′) deduces the falsity of determinism from his expansion and analysis of the elliptical sentence "Cicero can choose to kill Caesar", the philosopher who accepts (x) or (x*) does not assert or deduce the truth of determinism. In addition, a theory containing (x) or (x*) sits well with our normal use of the principle that every obligatory action is free whereas, as we shall see, the antideterminist who asserts (x′) cannot use this principle to show that some actions are not obligatory. If the antideterminist accepts (vi), the dictum that an action is obligatory only if it is free, then he should also say that if the agent is not free to perform an action, the agent has no obligation to perform that action. Moreover, in accordance with statement (viii) above, if an agent cannot choose to perform an action, he is not free to perform that action. So it follows, in accordance with a logical equivalent of (vi) above, that if an agent cannot choose to perform an action, he has no obligation to perform it. Earlier, however, we saw that an antideterminist who accepts (x′) is forced to say that we speak falsely whenever we say that an agent is not free to choose to perform an action. Consequently the antideterminist is not in a position to show that some actions are not obligatory by applying the principle which says that if an agent is not free to choose to perform an action, he has no obligation to perform it. Because he holds that every choice is possible or free, our antideterminist cannot validly relieve a person from the obligation to keep a promise by saying that the person *cannot* choose to keep his promise and therefore is not free to keep it. By contrast, the rival philosopher is not faced with this difficulty. Because he allows for the existence of impossible choices, he can show that certain actions are not obligatory by arguing that because Cicero cannot choose to kill Caesar, he cannot freely kill him, and because he cannot freely kill him, he has no duty to do so.

It is also worth remarking that since the antideterminist holds that every choice is possible, his test of whether
an action is free will in practice boil down to deciding
whether the two conditional conjuncts in the analysans of
"Cicero is free to kill Caesar" are true. For the antideterminist, any statement asserting the possibility of choice
will, so to speak, be automatically true whereas, by contrast, the opponent of the antideterminist will need, in
every case, to test all four conjuncts in the analysans of
"Cicero is free to kill Caesar" against experience before he
calls that statement true. This, of course, is connected with
the fact that the opponent of the antideterminist will
sometimes say that a person has no duty to perform an
action because that person cannot make a choice whereas
the antideterminist will say that a person has no duty to
perform an action only in cases where one of the two conditional conjuncts is false. The opponent of the antideterminist therefore provides us with more ways in which to
relieve a person of an obligation. All of this, of course, depends on viewing the antideterminist as a philosopher
who thinks that we should analyze "Cicero is free to kill
Caesar" as a conjunctive belief of the sort that I have been
attributing to him in this chapter.

The epistemology of corporatism is "made" for discussions of free will precisely because corporatism highlights
our need, when offering an analysis of free action, to as-
sess its impact on determinism and on the principle that
every obligatory act is causally necessitated by a free
choice. In other words, when we analyze free action and
free choice, we must, as corporatists, pay close attention
to the impact that our analysis has on these other beliefs.
If we decline to deny determinism because we think it true
or because we find it unclear, and if we seek a plausible
version of the principle that an agent has a duty to perform

a certain act only if he can choose to perform that act, then we should prefer the sort of conjunction that contains (x) or (x*) to the rival conjunction that contains (x'). I grant that the philosopher who is willing to jettison determinism may do so if he is willing to accept all of the consequences, but I have so far given two related arguments against taking that route. Not only have I argued that an antideterminist who accepts (x') implies that all choices are possible or free, which is contrary to our experience concerning choice or—if you prefer—to the way in which we normally speak about choice; I have also argued that taking this route prevents this antideterminist from saying that a person who cannot choose to keep a promise is relieved of a duty to keep it.

Now I come to simplicity, the third standard for comparing rival theories. When James speaks of it, he quotes the physicist Maxwell, who had once said that it would be poor scientific taste to choose the more complicated of two equally well evidenced theories. For Maxwell, considerations of simplicity would seem to enter a comparison of two theories only in cases where the evidence does not decide between our rival theories because they are equally well evidenced. If this is the way in which simplicity should enter our discussion of our rival theories, then, of course, it will not enter it at all if we think that application of James's principles of empiricism and conservativism shows that a theory containing (x) or (x*) is better evidenced than one containing (x'). But if simplicity must, for whatever reason, figure in comparing our two theories about free will, it would seem that the award for simplicity will go to the theory that contains (x'). For it bluntly and simply says that Cicero's not choosing to kill Caesar is not causally necessitated by any other event, whereas, by contrast, the theory that contains (x) or (x*) must, first of all, be accompanied by a defense of whichever path one takes: offering a criterion for being an appropriate precluder or offering a list of appropriate precluders. It must also be accompanied by a defense of the particular sort of precluder or the particular list that is offered. Therefore, it might be argued that the variety allowed by the theory containing (x) or (x*) makes it less simple than its rival. To this it may be replied that such variety is in accord with the experienced fact that people do, as a matter of fact, differ in their views about what makes a choice unfree and in their views about what makes it free because they differ as to what precluders or sorts of precluders of choice remove obligations. This difference constitutes part of the data that a theory of free will should take into account, even at the expense of becoming more complicated.

However, even if the test for simplicity should go against the theory favored by a philosopher, he might nevertheless say that the theory he favors is preferable. Why? Because the philosopher believes that his theory is preferable *on balance* to the other. I emphasize the words "on balance" in order to bring out an important feature of our thinking when we evaluate our two opposing theories on the basis of all three standards. Since we evaluate them on the basis of their capacity to organize experience, their capacity to preserve firmly held beliefs, and their simplicity, each theory may, so to speak, score points under each of these three headings and we may "trade off" points earned by a theory under one heading against points it loses under another heading. In my view the theory above that does not reject determinism comes out ahead of the theory that does because the former is more in accord with the fact that there are impossible choices, and with the belief that a person who cannot make a choice to perform an action does not have a duty to perform it. I say this even though it may be the case that the former theory is the less simple of the two.

I do not wish to conclude this section without pointing out that one of the virtues of comparing the rival theories as I have compared them is that this method of comparison helps us see why philosophers have debated this question for so long without arriving at a consensus. Although I have suggested that we think of the rival theories as similar to rival theories in, say, physics, I must admit, of course, that it is much harder to come to agreement about which of our theories is superior than it usually is in natural science. There are several reasons for this. One has to do with the fact that highly debatable moral beliefs play a part in the argument. Another has to do with the fact that philosophers and other human beings come to the problem with fixed ideas about determinism and free will that are very difficult for them to surrender and very difficult for others to persuade them to surrender. A third has to do with familiar difficulties surrounding the notion of meaning, difficulties that appear as soon as one asks the crucial question "What do we mean by saying 'Cicero is free to kill Caesar?'". All of this militates against achieving consensus about free will. Questions about morals, about metaphysics, and about meaning rarely elicit answers about which all philosophers agree, and so it is very unlikely that a theory of free will that contains statements of these three kinds will elicit the sort of agreement that we often achieve in what may be called other branches of science.

I want to remark here that although the theories I have compared here begin with a factual statement such as (o), contain a moral principle such as (i), factual statements about individuals such as (ii), (iii), and (iv), and a singular moral conclusion such as (v), all these statements might be replaced by others without altering the general comparison I have made. For example, someone else might have begun with the moral principle that everyone has a duty not to kill another person, have continued with the statement that Cain killed Abel, have inferred that Cain had a duty not to have killed Abel, and then have concluded that Cain could have not killed Abel before asserting the counterparts of the sentences from (vi) on. Therefore, my thesis is more general than one which merely says that the particular theory which runs from (o) through (x) or (x*) is superior to the particular one that runs from (o) through (x'). My thesis is that any theory which has the form of one running from (o) through (x) or (x*) is superior to one that has the form of one running from (o) through (x').[8]

4. The Problem of Ancestorial Determination

So far I have compared a kind of theory which, when it asserts (x) or (x*), neither asserts nor denies determinism with a kind of theory that does deny determinism by virtue of including (x'); I have argued that the former theory is superior by the epistemological standards I have used. I

---

[8] Of course, I might have enlarged the two rival theories by drawing further consequences from line (viii) in the argument presented earlier. Since that line is a conjunction of four statements, I might have deduced from it "If Cicero chooses to kill Caesar, he will kill him", "If Cicero chooses not to kill Caesar, he will not kill him", and "Cicero can choose not to kill Caesar". These other three statements would also have to lead to true experiential statements if the nonantideterministic theory were to be acceptable. And, of course, the antideterministic theorist and his rival would differ in their interpretation of "Cicero can choose not to kill Caesar", just as they differ in their interpretation of "Cicero can choose to kill Caesar". But it is obvious that the addition of these three statements to the two compared conjunctions would not affect my view that the nonantideterministic theory is preferable.

want to add, however, that I am happy that the theory I favor implies neither the truth nor the falsity of determinism, not because I am convinced that determinism is false or that it is true but because I am inclined to think that a theory of free will may be neutral on the subject. Of course, if I held with certain logical positivists—as I do not—that determinism is a meaningless metaphysical doctrine, I would be able to defend such neutrality with greater ease. I might also point out that if one were to say that determinism is meaningless or—with modesty or mock-modesty—say that one did not understand it, one might have difficulty in calling oneself a compatibilist or an incompatibilist. For if determinism were meaningless or if one did not comprehend it, it would be misleading for one to say with an incompatibilist that determinism logically implied the falsity of "Cicero could have killed Caesar" or with a compatibilist that it did not. This would be too much like saying that the meaningless sentence "Pirots karulize elatically" is compatible with this statement about Cicero, or that it is not. What I think I am entitled to say at this point is that a theory containing something like (x) or (x*) is superior to a theory containing (x'), that the former theory does not deny, contain, or imply determinism, and that certain defects of the latter originate in its antideterministic denial that choices are causally necessitated.

However, I cannot leave the matter there for the following reason. It has been argued that determinism not only implies that Cicero's not killing Caesar was causally necessitated or determined, but it also implies, using a term of Keith Lehrer's, that Cicero's not killing Caesar was *ancestorially determined*.[9] The point is that determinism logically

[9] Keith Lehrer, "An Empirical Disproof of Determinism?" in *Freedom and Determinism*, ed. K. Lehrer (New York: Random House, 1966), p. 200.

implies that the condition that causally determined Cicero's not killing Caesar was in turn causally determined by another earlier condition, which was causally determined by a still earlier condition, and so on, until at last we reach an earlier causally determining condition that existed before Cicero was born. And since causal necessitation or determination is a transitive relation, we may say that if one condition causally necessitates a second and that second causally necessitates a third, then the first causally necessitates the third. From this we may infer that Cicero's not killing Caesar was causally necessitated by a condition that existed before Cicero was born—a condition over which Cicero had no control. The question therefore arises: Is the statement that Cicero could have killed Caesar at a time when he did not kill him, logically compatible with the statement that Cicero's not killing Caesar was ancestorially determined? I should point out that my way of formulating the problem of compatibility as one concerned with the statements that Cicero did not *choose* to kill Caesar and that he could have *chosen* to do so is different from the way in which it is formulated by philosophers who focus on the statements that Cicero did not *kill* Caesar and that he could have killed him. Nevertheless, we may transfer certain things that have been said about the pair of statements concerned with action and possible action to the pair concerned with choice and possible choice. The problem about choice and possible choice may be formulated as follows: Is the statement that Cicero could have chosen to have killed Caesar at a time when he did not choose to kill him logically compatible with the statement that Cicero's not choosing to kill Caesar was ancestorially determined? Or, we may ask, is the statement that Cicero was free to choose to kill Caesar logically compatible with the statement that his not choosing to kill

109

him was causally necessitated by something beyond Cicero's control?

It happens, however, that this question does not seem to be discussable within the confines of a view advocated by Peter Van Inwagen, a leading exponent of the idea that determinism implies ancestorial determination and is therefore incompatible with free will. Nevertheless, it will be instructive to see why the problem is not discussable within the confines of this view. Van Inwagen has argued forcefully in an article and in a book[10] that free will and determinism are incompatible, by which he means that determinism *as he defines it* is incompatible with the thesis that we are able to *act* otherwise than we do. At one point in his argument he says that the hand of a man called "J" was not raised—that is, not up—at a certain time and that this action is an observable physical event on a par with a white cloth's not being blue and a warm liquid's not being cold. Van Inwagen then tries to show that if J's hand was not raised at that time and if determinism as he defines it is true, then J's hand could not have been raised at that time. In his article, "The Incompatibility of Free Will and Determinism", Van Inwagen's argument depends on his employing a version of determinism which says (a) that for every instant of time, there is an extralinguistically conceived proposition (not a sentence) that expresses the state of the entire *physical* world at that time; and (b) that if A and B are any propositions that express the state of the world at some instants, then the conjunction of A with the laws of *physics* entails B.[11] Van Inwagen says in his book

[10] The article is "The Incompatibility of Free Will and Determinism", *Philosophical Studies* 27 (1975): pp. 185–99; reprinted in *Free Will*, ed. G. Watson (Oxford: Oxford University Press, 1982), pp. 46–58. The book is *An Essay on Free Will.*

[11] See Van Inwagen, "Incompatibility", pp. 47–49.

that if an act by a person is incompatible with the state of the world before the person's birth taken together with the laws of nature, then it follows that that person could not have performed that act.[12] The reference to the state of the physical world before the person's birth shows that Van Inwagen thinks that a determinist believes that the person's behavior is ancestorially determined, and that the raising and nonraising of J's hand are *physical* events. I emphasize the word "physical" because I do not see how Van Inwagen's version of determinism can be applied to choices and nonchoices so long as it is, so to speak, physicalistically formulated.

To illustrate my point, I will suppose that Cicero did not choose to kill Caesar at the time some of Cicero's friends did choose to kill him. I think of this nonchoice as analogous to J's not raising his hand. The point I want to stress is that Van Inwagen's argument does not apply to Cicero's *not* choosing to kill Caesar simply because the conjunction of Van Inwagen's version of determinism and the statement that Cicero did not choose to kill Caesar at a certain time does not logically imply that Cicero could not have chosen to kill Caesar at that time. Van Inwagen's argument does not show that his version of determinism and Cicero's freedom of choice are incompatible unless choosing and not choosing are regarded as physical and the laws of physics are thought to contain the concepts *choose* and *not choose*. It is obvious, however, that "choose" and "not choose" do not appear among what Van Inwagen might call the linguistic expressions of the laws of physics, as they would have to if we were to deduce "Cicero could not have chosen to kill Caesar" from "Cicero did not choose to kill Caesar" in conjunction with

---

[12] Van Inwagen, *An Essay on Free Will*, p. 75.

Van Inwagen's formulation of determinism. Of course, if the expressions "choose" and "not choose" were completely eliminable in accordance with some reduction of psychology to physics, the situation would be different. But, so far as I know, such a reduction has not been accomplished.

Now I want to return to the very different views of Keith Lehrer, who, like Van Inwagen, is also concerned with free action rather than free choice. I find Lehrer's views congenial for a variety of reasons. First of all, he defends the compatibility of freedom of action and determinism, as well as the compatibility of freedom of action and ancestorial necessitation. In addition, I believe that his views on the relation between "Cicero could have killed Caesar" and determinism are transferable to the relation between "Cicero could have chosen to kill Caesar" and determinism. Moreover, Lehrer's formulation of determinism does not seem to require, as Van Inwagen's does, a commitment to an ontology of platonic propositions and a dependence on an unclarified application of the term "analytic" to propositions.[13] Finally, because Lehrer defends the compatibility of "Cicero is free to kill Caesar" and determinism by regarding them as empirical statements, his arguments may be formulated holistically. But because Lehrer is concerned with free action rather than free choice, I will first formulate his views about free action and determinism, and then transfer what he says about the relation between free action and determinism to the relation between free choice and determinism.

Lehrer's view, when applied to my illustration, is that "Cicero can kill Caesar", asserted at a time when Cicero does not kill Caesar, does not logically imply the two anti-

[13] Van Inwagen, "Incompatibility", pp. 49, 53.

deterministic statements "Cicero's not killing Caesar is not causally necessitated by anything" and "Cicero's not killing Caesar is not necessitated by an ancestorial cause". Lehrer's argument for his view is as follows. He says that a statement similar to "Cicero can kill Caesar", for example, "Cicero can lift his arm", may be supported empirically by showing that Cicero has, on similar occasions, lifted his arm. Lehrer then says that the evidence E which renders this statement highly probable, does not render "Cicero's not lifting his arm is not causally necessitated by anything" highly probable. Neither does E render "Cicero's not lifting his arm is not causally necessitated by an ancestorial cause" highly probable. Next, Lehrer appeals to a theorem of the calculus of probability which says that if one hypothesis logically implies another hypothesis, the evidence that renders the first highly probable will render the second at least as probable. On the basis of this, Lehrer concludes that "Cicero can lift his arm" does not logically imply "Cicero's not lifting his arm is not causally necessitated by anything"; nor does it logically imply "Cicero's not lifting his arm is not causally necessitated by an ancestorial cause". The point is that E does not render these two statements as probable as "Cicero can lift his arm".[14]

It seems to me that we may apply this sort of reasoning to the case of "Cicero can choose to kill Caesar", asserted when Cicero has not chosen to kill Caesar. Since determinism implies that Cicero's not choosing to kill Caesar is necessitated by an ancestorial cause, determinism will be logically incompatible with an expansion and analysis of

[14] Lehrer, "Empirical Disproof", pp. 198–202. I am aware of certain differences between "Cicero can lift his arm" and "Cicero can kill Caesar" that are connected with the fact that Cicero must have lifted his arm on many occasions but never killed Caesar. However, I believe that we may disregard these differences in the present context.

"Cicero can choose to kill Caesar" that reads "Cicero's not choosing not to kill Caesar is not necessitated by an ancestorial cause". Therefore, this is an expansion-cum-analysis which is to be avoided by one who wishes to avoid contradicting determinism. It should be noticed, however, that none of the expansions-cum-analyses that I have preferred say that "Cicero can choose to kill Caesar" should be expanded in this antideterministic way. It should also be noticed that no one of them logically implies "Cicero's not choosing to kill Caesar is not necessitated by an ancestorial cause". Therefore, no expansion-cum-analysis of "Cicero can choose to kill Caesar" of the kind I propose will imply the falsity of determinism.

It is worth remarking that the failure of "Cicero can kill Caesar" to imply that Cicero's not killing Caesar is not causally or ancestorially determined may be seen more easily if we note the following. Saying that it is not causally determined is equivalent to saying that it is not determined by A, by B, by C, and so on whereas saying that it is not ancestorially determined is equivalent to saying that Cicero's not killing Caesar was not caused by X, or X was not caused by Y, or Y was not caused by Z, and so on until we reach a cause prior to Cicero's birth.

Although the question of ancestorial determination is discussed by Lehrer while considering its relation to the possibility of acting otherwise, his method of doing so may be, as I have said, transferred to the possibility of *choosing* otherwise. If it is transferred in this way after we have stated how to support our statement that Cicero could have made a choice he did not make, I see no obstacle to dealing with it by analogy to the way in which Lehrer deals with the possibility of action. In other words, the evidence for "Cicero could have chosen to kill Caesar" will not render highly probable "Cicero's not choosing to kill Caesar was not causally necessitated by anything" or "Cicero's not choosing to kill Caesar was not ancestorially determined". And this will show that "Cicero could have chosen to kill Caesar" does not logically imply either of these statements.

I want to add something that perhaps I should have emphasized more in earlier parts of this study, namely, that for anyone who analyzes free action or free will as I do in the four-conjunct sentence (viii) and who continues the argument as I do to (x) or (x*), the problem of free will versus determinism boils down to the problem of free choice versus determinism. Therefore I might have focused on moral principles that are principles governing choices and I might have given illustrations of such moral principles by saying things like "All citizens ought *to choose* to kill tyrants" instead of "All citizens ought *to kill* tyrants". In that case I would have needed to consider only the relationship between "Cicero ought to choose to kill Caesar" and "Cicero can choose to kill Caesar", and I would have needed to ask only what the latter sentence means, without having to ask what it means to say "Cicero can kill Caesar". This would have relieved me of the need to analyze free action as opposed to free choice but not the need to compare conjunctions about choice when evaluating rival theories as I do.

The fact that the possibility of choosing otherwise is central to my discussion of antideterminism shows why Van Inwagen's attempt to undermine Lehrer's view about free action does not affect my view about free *choice* in relation to determinism. Van Inwagen tries to undermine Lehrer's argument for the compatibility of free will and determinism as applied to actions by showing that Lehrer, by using an argument like the one he uses to show the compatibility of free will and determinism, would have to say that a certain theory (M), which entails "that no one can act otherwise than he does" but which is not the doctrine of determinism, is compatible with free will when in fact it is not. The theory (M) says:

> When any human being is born, the Martians implant in his brain a tiny device—one that is undetectable by any observational technique we have at our disposal, though it is not *in principle* undetectable—which contains a "program" for that person's entire life: whenever that person must make a decision, the device *causes* him to decide one way or the other according to the requirements of a table of instructions that were incorporated into the structure of the device before that person was conceived.[15]

The reader will note that the theory contains the word "decision", a word that might suggest that the theory is about choices, but I believe that Van Inwagen wants to say something about the causation of physical events such as the raising and nonraising of J's hand in the light of his statement that (M) entails that no one can *act* otherwise than he does, and in the light of his reference to physical actions and physical laws in his statement that determinism implies that J's unraised hand *must be* unraised. Van Inwagen's criticism of Lehrer is that Lehrer, because of his argument to show that "J could have raised his hand" does not imply the falsity of determinism, must say that the evidence E renders "J could have raised his hand" highly probable whereas it does not render the denial of (M) highly probable, and therefore that "J could have raised his hand" does not logically imply that (M) is false. But Van Inwagen thinks that "J could have raised his hand"

[15] Van Inwagen, *An Essay on Free Will*, p. 109.

does imply that (M) is false, and therefore that Lehrer's defense of the compatibility of free action and determinism is questionable.

It seems to me that Van Inwagen's argument may be correct as applied to things such as J's not raising his hand or Cicero's not killing Caesar, but I do not believe that it is applicable to Cicero's not choosing to kill Caesar. I say this not only because of what Van Inwagen draws as a logical consequence of (M), namely, that no one can *act* otherwise than he does, but also because, as we have seen, he must regard determinism as a doctrine that applies to such physical things as J's not raising his hand but not to such things as Cicero's not choosing to kill Caesar. By contrast, I think that Lehrer's version of determinism *is* applicable to nonchoices and choices, and that when it is applied to them, it is not vulnerable to Van Inwagen's criticism. In the light of this, I am strongly inclined to say that Lehrer's version of determinism, even with its implication of ancestorial necessitation, is not incompatible with the statement that Cicero could have chosen to kill Caesar, especially when that statement is construed as I construe it in (x) and (x*). I am therefore strongly inclined to say that this makes it easier for me to favor the conjunctive theory above that contains (x) or (x*). It will be recalled that the conjunction I favor does not contain the principle of determinism nor imply that it is true. However, if determinism could be shown to be false or incompatible with "Cicero can choose to kill Caesar", that would remove certain objections to the theory that contains (x') and therefore make it more difficult for me to come down as hard as I do in favor of the theory containing (x) or (x*).

117

Concluding Remarks on
Moral Belief and
Free Will

1. Two Questionable Inferences

In formulating the rival theories compared in the previous chapter, I have said that they contain the conjunct (vi), "Whoever ought to kill a person is free to kill that person". And although I have pointed out that the grounds for asserting this may differ because I treat this as a moral principle whereas others treat it as a different kind of truth, I have not focused on this dispute over the status of (vi) while concentrating on the dispute between those who accept (x′) rather than (x) or (x*). I want therefore to emphasize here that in my view some philosophers make two mistakes. They not only think that we must accept (x′) rather than (x) or (x*) but they treat (vi) as a rational principle, conceptual truth, or synthetic necessary truth and therefore think that "Cicero is free to kill Caesar" logically follows from "Cicero ought to kill Caesar". In my view, their notion that "Ought" logically implies "Free" is just as faulty as the notion that "Free" *must* be construed as it is in (x′).

This is a good place at which to reiterate and to elaborate on what I say earlier in chapter 1, section 2, about the analytic and the synthetic. Because I believe that the con-

ventional distinction between analytic and synthetic statements is unclear, I think that saying that (vi) is analytic or
that it is synthetic is unclear. Yet I also think that the distinction which some philosophers have in mind when they
use the terms "analytic" and "synthetic" coincides fairly
well in extension with the distinction between true statements that we are extremely reluctant to surrender and
those we are less reluctant to surrender. Therefore, when
I criticize those who think that "Cicero ought to kill Caesar" logically implies "Cicero is free to kill Caesar", or that
it analytically implies it, I want to be understood as saying
that the principle underlying this implication is not one
that we are as reluctant to surrender as we are to surrender the principles of formal logic, substitution-instances
of them, or statements such as "Every brother is a male",
"Every bachelor is unmarried", or "Whatever is colored
is extended". Moreover, when I say that the statement
"Whoever ought to kill a person is free to kill that person"
is a moral principle, I believe I strengthen my claim that it
is a principle which is more readily abandoned than those
that I have just listed. I strengthen my claim because, gen-
erally speaking, moral principles are more likely to be dis-
agreed about, surrendered, or revised than those I have
listed.

Having said this, I think it fair to add that sometimes, in
an effort to put myself in the position of those who do not
share my views on the analytic and the synthetic, I use—
perhaps it might be said that I lapse into using—the language of philosophers who not only distinguish sharply
between analytic and synthetic statements but who believe that there are synthetic necessary truths or synthetic
a priori truths and who hold that (vi) is such a truth. For
them, the concept of being obligatory does not contain the

concept of being free as the concept of being a brother contains the concept of being a male, and yet they say that it is a necessary truth that every obligatory act is free. To advocates of such a view—in what may seem to some to amount to excessive fairness or generosity—I say the following: Even if I were to accept your dubious views on the analytic and the synthetic, and even if I were to accept your dubious view that there are synthetic necessary truths, I would deny that "Whoever ought to kill a person is free to kill that person" is a synthetic necessary truth because I think it is quite different from "Nothing that is red all over is green all over"—different insofar as I can conceive an obligatory act which is not free whereas I cannot conceive a thing which is red all over and green all over. Therefore, I say to my philosophical opponent: Even if I were to step into your philosophical shoes, I would not assert that "Whoever ought to kill a person is free to kill that person" is a conceptual truth, a synthetic necessary truth, or a synthetic a priori truth and therefore immune to surrender or revision.

I want to underscore the significance of my view that "Ought" morally implies "Free" is based on the *moral* principle "Every obligatory action is free". Since my view is based on that moral principle, it will be comparatively easy for philosophers and ordinary persons to disagree about it. I have said that someone could, for example, call an action obligatory if and only if it is prescribed by a moral principle of the form "Every action of kind D is obligatory" and not accept the moral principle that every obligatory action is free, which is not of that form. Such a person might assert, without thinking that he was violating some unsurrenderable truth, that an action is of kind D and therefore obligatory even though it is not free. Thus, after concluding that Cicero's killing of Caesar is obligatory by deducing it from a moral principle and descriptive premises, he might reject the idea that Cicero's being obligated to kill Caesar implied that Cicero's killing of Caesar was free.

What I have just been saying shows something important about the two main inferences that I have challenged in this study. In a certain respect, the crucial mistaken step that some philosophers take from "Cicero's action is obligatory" to "Cicero's action is free" is like their crucial step from "Cicero's action is free" to "Cicero's not choosing to perform the action is not caused by any event". The first step seems necessary to some philosophers because they think it rests on a truth that cannot be abandoned; they think that the second step is also necessary in some sense. But if they interpret "Cicero can choose to kill Caesar" as meaning the same as "Cicero's not choosing to kill Caesar is not causally necessitated", they err if they think that this last elliptical statement *must* be expanded and analyzed into "Cicero's not choosing to kill Caesar is not necessitated *by anything*". This second, fallacious "must" takes them from an incomplete sentence to its allegedly unique completion. Their mistake is like the mistake of believing that the sentence "Tom is tall" *must* be elliptical for "Tom is taller than most people in his school" and *not* elliptical for "Tom is taller than most people" when in fact "Tom is tall" may be completed in either way, or in one of many other ways, depending on what the speaker has in mind and on what other statements he makes in conjunction with "Tom is tall". Therefore, as soon as one recognizes that "Cicero can choose to kill Caesar" may be interpreted by some users of the language in the manner of (x) or (x*) rather than in the manner of (x'), one may see the advantages of adopting (x) or (x*) and the disadvantages of adopting (x').

121

2. The Two Questionable Inferences
Made by James

Some readers may be surprised by my use of what may be called a pragmatic theory of knowledge in order to support the view that a belief in free will does not logically imply that the doctrine of determinism or universal causation is false—surprised because they know that the pragmatist William James came to a very different conclusion on the same subject. For this reason I want to say why I disagree with James's main conclusions about free will even though I agree with some of the epistemological standards that he used in coming to them. The simple explanation is that James seems to have made both of the mistakes I have discussed in the last section. First of all, he says in reply to one of his critics: "*Ought* rationally involves *can*"; and it was, James says, to avoid denying this rational involvement that he adopted indeterminism.[1] Secondly, he rejects what he calls "soft determinism" because it leads to what he calls the evasive conclusion that "sometimes we are free and sometimes we are not".[2]

I have said enough about the claim that ought rationally involves can to show why I think it a mistaken claim. But to understand why James made it, we should note that in some of his other writings, James held that there are so-called rational beliefs which may be established by merely examining what he called "ideal conceptions". Among these are the belief that 2 + 2 = 4, the principles of formal logic, and the belief that no white thing is black; these are the beliefs to which James likened his belief that ought involves can. In "The Dilemma of Determinism" (1884) he

[1] James, *The Will to Believe*, p. 444.
[2] Ibid., p. 117.

seems to have treated the belief that ought involves can as he treated "No white thing is black" in his *Principles of Psychology* (1890), and so he seems to have regarded this belief as immutable and not rejectable by an appeal to any kind of experience. I believe that in later writings James diverged from the view of necessary truth that he adopted in the *Principles*, but in "The Dilemma of Determinism" he seemed prepared to say that the dictum "Ought involves can" is as immutable and as immune to revision as any other so-called necessary truth.[3] His argument against determinism in that paper began with the statement that we sometimes regret the performance of certain actions. And, he continued, if we regret the performance of them, we think they ought not to have been performed; from which it follows necessarily, James holds, that it was possible for them not to have been performed. But determinism denies that it was possible for these performed actions not to have been performed, and therefore James rejects determinism because he treats "Ought involves can" as a truth that he thinks he must accept whereas, obviously, he did not feel compelled to accept determinism. His mistake here, I think, was to reverse the view of militant determinists, to freeze "Ought involves can" into an unrejectable truth while rejecting determinism with comparative ease.

Having said this, I want to reaffirm my own acceptance of the moral principle that a choice is obligatory only if it is free as well as the moral principle that an action is obligatory only if it is free. My disagreement with James is therefore over the status of these principles: I regard them as surrenderable in the light of sensory and emotional experience whereas he does not. But at this point the reader

[3] For a fuller discussion of James's views on this matter, see my *Science and Sentiment in America* (New York: Oxford University Press, 1972), chap. 8, esp. pp. 210–16.

may well remark that a thoroughgoing holist regards all principles—even those of logic—as surrenderable in the light of experience, and therefore may wonder why I insist that the principles connecting obligation and freedom are moral rather than logical. After all, it might be pointed out, if logical principles are surrenderable in the light of experience, then a logical version of either principle that connects obligation with freedom would be surrenderable; so why insist that these principles are *moral*? My reply is that I think moral principles are more likely to be abandoned than logical principles when experience rebuffs a conjunctive theory that contains both kinds of principles, just as I think that the physical principles in such a theory are more likely to be abandoned than the logical principles in it. Furthermore, the principles connecting obligation and freedom look more like statements in the Decalogue than they look like the principle of the syllogism.

Now I turn to James's second mistake from my point of view. In "The Dilemma of Determinism", he criticizes those who hold on to determinism while affirming that we have free will. Some of them he calls "soft determinists", and he condemns them as evasive, as I have said. But why does he call them evasive when they define "free action" as "acting without external constraint" in their effort to make determinism compatible with freedom? James's answer seems to be that it is evasive to offer a definition according to which it turns out that we are sometimes free and sometimes not. He thinks the issue between determinism and its opposite *must* be drawn in a way that does not permit this conclusion; but this seems mistaken to me because one of the conditions that I think a theory of free will should satisfy is that it preserve the truth of our belief that some choices can be made and others not.

It should be evident now why I think that one may agree

with certain parts of James's epistemology and yet disagree with his views on free will. James's idea that a good scientific theory economically marries novel experience with past belief does not logically dictate which position one should take on the issues that concern me in this study, but I would like to call attention to two ironies connected with this idea. First of all, I think my view of the relation between "Ought" and "Can" is more in keeping with a central feature of James's pragmatism than James's view of this relation was. I mean that it is more in keeping with James's moral pluralism and with his readiness in some of his writings to reject the unacceptable rationalism that I see in the idea that "*ought* rationally involves *can*". Secondly, I think that my view on free choice is in keeping with James's idea that a good theory should derange common sense and previous belief as little as possible whereas James's view that *all* choices are free requires a considerable derangement of common sense or of previous belief.

Although I believe that an antideterministic theory or conjunction of the kind that James favored is inferior to its rival in the various ways I have just discussed, I do not claim to have logically demonstrated its falsity. I can well imagine that the antideterminist discussed in the previous chapter might stick to his theory on grounds that deserve serious consideration; indeed, I have given some of those grounds serious consideration. And I recognize that an antideterminist is not logically bound to interpret "Cicero can choose to kill Caesar" as I have interpreted it. I do not insist that the expansion-cum-analysis that leads from (ix) to (x) or to (x*) in the previous chapter is the only one that may be offered by one who agrees that "Cicero can choose to kill Caesar" may be expanded and analyzed so that it is replaced by a sentence beginning with the words "Cicero's not choosing to kill Caesar is not causally necessitated".

The relativism or the pluralism that I espouse permits other persons to add other expressions to this elliptical sentence in accordance with their moral beliefs, including the expression "by any other event". But I have pointed to difficulties that accompany this last addition, especially the difficulty of being unable to assert that because a certain choice is impossible for a person to make, he cannot perform a certain action and therefore is not obligated to perform it. This means that the antideterminist's analysis of "free" prevents us from asserting many moral truths that I for one accept.

I stress this because it allows me to refer to a statement by James that I find very interesting and relevant to what I have been saying. He says in "The Dilemma of Determinism":

> The principle of causality, for example,—what is it but a postulate, an empty name covering simply a demand that the sequence of events shall some day manifest a deeper kind of belonging of one thing with another than the mere arbitrary juxtaposition which now phenomenally appears? It is as much an altar to an unknown god as the one that Saint Paul found at Athens. All our scientific and philosophic ideals are altars to unknown gods. Uniformity is as much so as is free-will. If this be admitted, we can debate on even terms. But if any one pretends that while freedom and variety are, in the first instance, subjective demands, necessity and uniformity are something altogether different, I do not see how we can debate at all.[4]

This passage shows that James thought that the human inclination to accept the principle of causality is on a par with the inclination to believe in free will. In saying this he

[4] James, *The Will to Believe*, p. 116.

was resisting the idea that the latter inclination was "subjective" whereas the former was not, and that the former was therefore the only inclination that should be respected. Indeed, he went on to insist that the belief in free will is even more respectable than the belief in causality, and that because our "ought"-statements rationally involve "can"-statements, we must believe in a variety of free will that contradicts the principle of causality or determinism. My own view is that we should respect the inclination to accept determinism by settling on a theory which, while it does not accept determinism, does not reject it either; and that we should respect the inclination to believe in free will by trying to construe that belief in a way that does not conflict with determinism. However, I not only put determinism and the belief that we have free will on a par, I also put the principle that links "Ought" with "Can" on that par. I find it curious that James, while saying that "all our scientific and philosophic ideals are altars to unknown gods", should have failed to recognize this. In my view, none of the three beliefs—determinism, the belief that we have free will, and the belief that a choice is obligatory only if we can make it—is immune to revision or rejection in the light of experience. That is why I shy away from calling them necessary, analytic, or synthetic a priori, and that is why I do not think that a singular statement that a choice is morally obligatory analytically implies a statement that the choice is free, even though I happen to believe that the former statement morally implies the latter.

3. A Remark on Aristotle

The role of moral belief in the discussion of free will may be illuminated by considering Aristotle's discussion of voluntariness. He says at the beginning of Book 3 of his *Nicomachean Ethics* that there is some doubt as to whether actions done through fear of a worse alternative are voluntary or involuntary, and I agree. But my doubt about this does not derive merely from a doubt about the meaning of the word "voluntary" that can be resolved in the abstract without attention to the moral belief that every obligatory action is free. In other words, when we ask whether an action done through fear of a worse alternative is not voluntary in Aristotle's sense or not free in mine, I think our answer will depend on whether we are prepared to say that if it is not voluntary or not free, then it is not obligatory. In analyzing the concept of voluntariness we should not include the concept of obligatoriness in the analysis but we should analyze it in such a way as to preserve the truth of the moral principle that a nonvoluntary action is not obligatory. Indeed, this principle is the main context of the term "nonvoluntary" to which we must attend when trying to resolve the doubt mentioned above. Aristotle's doubt whether a person acts voluntarily when he has done something base out of fear of doing something worse cannot be resolved without taking a stand on the moral question of whether such a person should be relieved of his duty not to do that base thing. For example, suppose we ask with Aristotle whether a man acts voluntarily when he breaks a promise to do something because a tyrant has threatened to kill everyone in his family if he keeps his promise. In keeping with what I have said elsewhere, I think that to test whether this man's not keeping his promise is voluntary we should ask whether he has a duty to keep his promise under the circumstances; and if our answer is that he has no duty to keep it, this shows that we regard his failure to keep his promise as not voluntary.

I want to reiterate that I do not think we can analyze the

freedom of an act without attention to a moral context; we cannot analyze this attribute merely by thinking about the attribute in isolation. In order to specify what sense of "voluntary" or "free" we are trying to analyze, we must at least say something like "We are trying to analyze the attribute of freedom which is the sense of 'free' in the moral statement 'Whoever ought to perform an act is free to perform it' or in its equivalent 'Every obligatory act is free'". And I cannot think of *descriptive* contexts of the word "free" that serve this purpose as well. One might appeal to singular descriptive contexts such as "Socrates' drinking of hemlock was free", but such contexts are often controversial, not always accepted by all interested parties, and therefore not likely to help us specify with consensus at the beginning of our inquiry what sense of "free" we have in mind. Even though "free" is a descriptive predicate, we cannot at that point adduce many totally descriptive statements in which it appears, descriptive statements whose truth all parties are sure they want to preserve when analyzing "free". That is why the moral statement "Every obligatory act is free" is so important a context for us when we seek to analyze free will.

It is true that logical reflection on the relationship between causal possibility and causal necessity may prompt a philosopher to hold that the elliptical "Cicero can choose to kill Caesar" should, in a first step, be interpreted as meaning the same as the elliptical "Cicero's not choosing to kill Caesar is not causally necessitated", but logical reflection will not be enough to determine how to complete or expand such an elliptical denial of necessitation. Completing it will require the philosopher to take into account a moral principle, namely, (vi), that will play an important part in his moving, as in the previous chapter, from (ix) to (x) or to (x*) as opposed to (x'). A logical equivalent of this moral principle—its contrapositive—will determine the conditions under which we are not obligated to perform an act. If it says in conjunction with (x) that we are not obligated to perform an act if our choosing to perform the act is precluded by what I have called an absolute precluder, then we are taken off the hook of duty whenever our choice *is* so precluded. But if we construe the contrapositive of this moral principle as saying that we are not obligated to perform an act if our choice is precluded by either an absolute or nonabsolute precluder, then we will be claiming that additional causes of not making that choice—additional precluders—will also get us off the hook. To see what I have in mind here, suppose that fear of performing an action (a nonabsolute precluder) and being attacked by a choice-preventing disease (an absolute precluder) are both regarded as precluders that relieve us of an obligation to perform the action. A moral judge should not increase the number of such appropriate precluders without limit if he wishes to avoid saying that *every* cause of nonchoice will get us off the hook of duty, that *tout comprendre* is *tout pardonner*. My view is that only some precluders of choice do this and are therefore appropriate; I believe that the judgment as to exactly which precluders are appropriate may vary from moral code to moral code.

4. In Reply to Certain Objections

The fact that I sometimes say that a person who cannot make a choice is excused from an obligation to make it may lead a reader to object that not every condition that excuses a person from making a choice is one that causally necessitates his not making it. The following illustration has been offered to me in defense of this view. A certain X has promised to return a gun he has borrowed from Y, who, while in a rage, asks X to return the gun immediately so that Y may kill Z. In some versions of the illustration it is said that Z is X's beloved grandmother in order to make it easier for X to break his promise, but this is of no great moment once it is added that X's *moral* concern for Z causes X to choose to keep the gun and therefore to break his promise to choose to return it to Y. We may also be told that X's concern for Z provides X with a moral excuse for not choosing to return the gun. It is then said that X's moral concern is a condition which causally necessitates X's choosing as he does and therefore not choosing as his promise requires; and it is said in opposition to my view that this excusatory condition does not imply that the person cannot choose to return the gun. It is said that X can choose to return the gun even though X's not choosing to return the gun is causally necessitated by X's concern for Z, whether Z is X's grandmother or not.

To this objection I think we may respond as follows: How can it be said that although X's concern for Z causally necessitated X's not choosing to return the gun, X could have chosen to return the gun? It would seem that if X's concern for Z causally necessitated X's not choosing to return the gun to Y, then X could *not* have chosen to return the gun in one, and that the relevant, sense of "could". It does not matter that there is another sense of "could" according to which X could have chosen to return the gun. A man who is able to choose to return borrowed things, to hand them back to their lenders, might well be unable to make a choice to do so while under a hypnotic spell. The distinction between these two uses of "can" is often made in the literature on free will.

In my view, the application of the word "moral" to X's concern for Z or to his excuse does not cut the ice that the objector wants it to cut so long as the objector maintains that this moral concern causally necessitated X's not choosing to hand over the gun. Having said this, I want to emphasize that when we say that X's having an attack of epileptic automatism and X's being morally concerned about Z are *both* conditions that relieve X of the obligation to keep a promise, we indicate acceptance of the following two moral statements: (1) Since X's having an attack of epileptic automatism caused X not to choose to return the borrowed gun, X had no obligation to make that promised choice; and (2) Since X's moral concern for Z caused X not to choose to return the borrowed gun, X had no obligation to make that promised choice. However, if X were not to choose to return the gun because Z owed X money that X thought he would lose if Z were killed, we might wonder about this as an excuse because we might wonder about the acceptability of the following moral statement: (3) Since X's concern for recovering money that Z owed him caused X not to choose to return the gun, X had no obligation to make that promised choice. In general, the objection stated above merely shows that we may excuse a failure to choose to do something that is presumably obligatory in cases where one moral principle, such as the obligation to choose to do something that will probably save a life, takes precedence over the principle requiring us to choose to keep promises. But the objection certainly does not show that in such cases a person may be excused from making a choice when he *can* make it. If he cannot make a choice because he obeys the principle that takes precedence, he is excused even though he can *usually* make the sort of choice in question. After all, the agent in the earlier illustration from Aristotle can usually keep his promise even though we might say that he cannot when a tyrant has threatened to kill his family if he does not.

132

I might add that it is not altogether clear to me what the objector means when he says that X's *moral* concern for Z caused X not to choose to return the borrowed gun. But if he means that X's belief that Z ought not to be killed caused X not to choose to return the gun, it is clear why we may regard statements (1) and (2) above as similar. That X's belief that Z ought not to be killed is a *moral* belief does not militate against my view that the statement "X's belief that Z ought not to be killed caused X not to choose to return the gun" is a descriptive causal statement, just as "X's being in a hypnotic trance caused X not to choose to return the gun" is. The former is a descriptive statement which says that believing a moral statement caused a person not to make a certain choice whereas the latter says that being in a different sort of state had a similar effect. In both cases we may say that the person could not make that choice in a sense that leads us to excuse the person who does not make it.

I emphasize my liberalism or pluralism about which precluders are excusatory as well as my preference in chapter 6 for a theory that neither contains nor implies determinism partly because Isaiah Berlin has said in presumed disagreement with me: "I do not claim to have refuted the conclusions of determinism; but neither do I see why we need to be driven towards them. Neither the idea of historical explanation as such, nor respect for scientific method, seems to me to entail them. This sums up my disagreements with Professor Ernest Nagel, Professor Morton White, Mr. E. H. Carr, the classical determinists, and their modern disciples".[5] I wish to say in reply that I do not think that the idea of historical explanation or respect for scientific method "entails" or logically implies the conclu-

[5] Berlin, *Four Essays on Liberty*, p. xxxvii.

133

sions of determinism, and in the present work I have taken special care to avoid saying anything like that. Determinism, I have said, is *not* logically implied by any of the statements that appear in the sequence (o) through (x) or (x*) in chapter 6. For it should be noted that the statements "If Cicero chooses to kill Caesar, he will kill him" and "If Cicero chooses not to kill Caesar, he will not kill him" do not logically imply determinism simply by virtue of being causal conditional statements. Individual statements of causal connection between events do not logically imply that every event has a cause. And because the antideterminist cannot correctly claim that (x') is inescapably *the* expansion of (ix) above, he does not demonstrate the truth of antideterminism. Furthermore, I think, as I have said earlier, that we may apply an argument of Lehrer to choices in order to refute the view that determinism is incompatible with free choice because it implies that choices are determined by conditions that antedate the birth of the agent.

I know of no philosophical argument which demonstrates that determinism is false on the ground that it is incompatible with what we should say and think about choices. Nor do I know of any philosophical argument which successfully shows that a conditional statement such as "Moore would have walked a mile in twenty minutes this morning if he had chosen" is not a causal statement. Although I think we must add to this causal conditional statement the statement that Moore could have chosen to walk a mile in twenty minutes this morning if we wish to analyze "Moore could have walked a mile in twenty minutes this morning", I have tried to show why this added statement need not lead us to deny determinism. In my view, certain efforts to show that "Moore would have walked a mile in twenty minutes this morning if he had chosen" is *not* causal have been unsuccessful; and so have certain other efforts to show that "Moore could have chosen to walk a mile in twenty minutes this morning" contradicts determinism. If I am right on both of these matters, I have shown that determinism may be protected from some of its critics but I have certainly not demonstrated—nor have I tried to demonstrate—that it is true. Instead, I have holistically defended a theory about free will which implies neither the truth or the falsity of determinism and I have given what I regard as good holistic or corporatist reasons for preferring that theory to the anti-deterministic rival with which I have compared it. In my view these theories confront each other as two rival theories in natural science do and I have tried to show that one of them is superior when we take into account the sorts of considerations that we should take into account when evaluating such theories.